Design Ed

Connecting Learning Science Research to Practice

ANGELA ELKORDY
AND AYN KENEMAN

International Society for Technology in Education
PORTLAND, OREGON • ARLINGTON, VIRGINIA

Design Ed
Connecting Learning Science Research to Practice
Angela Elkordy and Ayn Keneman

Editor: *Emily Reed*
Developmental Editor: *Lynda Gansel*
Copy Editor: *Karstin Painter*
Indexer: *Wendy Allex*
Book Design and Production: *Kim McGovern*
Cover Design: *Edwin Ouellette*

Library of Congress Cataloging-in-Publication Data

Names: Elkordy, Angela, author. | Keneman, Ayn F., author.
   Title: Design ed : connecting learning science research to practice / Angela Elkordy and Ayn Keneman.
   Description: First edition. | Portland, Oregon : International Society for Technology in Education, [2019] | Includes bibliographical references and index.
   Identifiers: LCCN 2019018795 (print) | LCCN 2019981019 (ebook) | ISBN 9781564847492 (paperback) | ISBN 9781564847522 (pdf) | ISBN 9781564847515 (epub) | ISBN 9781564847508 (mobi)
   Subjects: LCSH: Instructional systems—Design. | Learning, Psychology of. | Education—Aims and objectives.
   Classification: LCC LB1028.38 .E45 2019 (print) | LCC LB1028.38 (ebook) | DDC 371.3—dc23
   LC record available at https://lccn.loc.gov/2019018795
   LC ebook record available at https://lccn.loc.gov/2019981019

First Edition
ISBN: 978-1-56484-749-2

Ebook version available.

Printed in the United States of America

ISTE® is a registered trademark of the International Society for Technology in Education.

About ISTE

The International Society for Technology in Education (ISTE) is the premier nonprofit organization serving educators and education leaders committed to empowering connected learners in a connected world. ISTE serves more than 100,000 education stakeholders throughout the world.

ISTE's innovative offerings include the ISTE Conference & Expo, one of the biggest, most comprehensive edtech events in the world—as well as the widely adopted ISTE Standards for learning, teaching and leading in the digital age and a robust suite of professional learning resources, including webinars, online courses, consulting services for schools and districts, books, and peer-reviewed journals and publications. Visit iste.org to learn more.

Related ISTE Titles

Edtech for the K–12 Classroom: ISTE Readings on How, When and Why to Use Technology (2018)

Dive into UDL: Immersive Practices to Develop Expert Learners, by Kendra Grant and Luis Perez (2018)

To see all books available from ISTE, please visit iste.org/Books.

About the Authors

Angela Elkordy, Ph.D., is chair and assistant professor, learning sciences, and program director for learning technologies at National Louis University in the Chicago area. Her writing has appeared in numerous platforms and publications, including books such as *Foundation of Digital Badges, Micro-Credentials,* and *Gamify Literacy*. Her research focuses on the learning sciences, design and technology, teacher learning, and instructional design.

Ayn Keneman, Ed.D., is an associate professor in the National College of Education faculty, early childhood education, at National Louis University, where she teaches courses in early childhood education, literacy instruction, human development, and technology. She is president of the Organization of Teacher Educators of Literacy, a special interest group of the International Literacy Association. Keneman's research on struggling readers led to the publication of her book *Literacy Leadership to Support Reading Improvement*.

Acknowledgments

Learning, at its core, is social. Our ideas are built upon and informed by our interactions with others. We wish to extend our gratitude for the many conversations with our colleagues at National Louis University and beyond, which helped us to build our ideas. In particular, Angela would like to thank National College of Education's dean, Dr. Robert Muller and director, Dr. Stuart Carrier, for championing the idea of learning sciences-informed practices for our National Louis University educator preparation, and Director of Advanced Professional Programs, Dr. Kathy Pluymert, for continuing to grow the vision. Angela would also like to extend appreciation to colleagues, thought partners, and friends Diane Salmon, Shani Beth-Halachmy, Marjorie Leon, and Nicole Zumpano. Thank you for your generosity of spirit and great ideas! Ayn would also like to thank University of Virginia's Glen Bull, who currently provides leadership for the National Technology Leadership Coalition, a consortium of national teacher educator associations and national educational technology associations, for his mentorship over the last several years.

We would like to extend heartfelt appreciation to Kristin Fontichiaro, assistant professor in the School of Information at the University of Michigan, and to the ISTE team, including the lovely Valerie Witte and our wonderful editor, Emily Reed, supported by Lynda Gansel and others. Thanks so much for unwrapping and clarifying our vision of this text! Sending much gratitude to Amy Hall, librarian and instructor at National Louis University, for working her APA magic on references (changes and errors are ours). Also, thank you very much to our earliest reviewers who shared excellent feedback which was so helpful in structuring this ambitious work. We appreciate you!.

We extend special appreciation to the educators with whom we work—you inspire us. Thank you for sharing your great ideas and questions—and for many in Angela's classes, for sharing your work in this book (changes and errors are ours). Also, thank you very much to our earliest reviewers who shared excellent feedback which was so helpful in structuring this ambitious work. We appreciate you!

Dedication

This book is dedicated to our students, both preservice and practicing educators. You motivate us with your passion and dedication to reach every learner. You amaze us with your phenomenal abilities and constant curiosity for inquiry into learning!

Angela sends a special thank you and much appreciation to family cheerleaders— Del, Dad, S'mum, Zack, Sara, Moaaz, Brian, and Sarah—who made this writing possible with their love, humor, and encouragement.

Contents

PART I
Lessons from the Field: Learning, Design, and Technology

CHAPTER 1
Educators, Learning Design, and the Science of Learning 13

Contents

Introduction

Everything should be made as simple as it can be, but not simpler.
— ALBERT EINSTEIN

Hello, reader! You may be wondering if this is a book for you. If you educate others —or care about teaching and learning—then yes, this book is for you! This book is a salute to the complexity and importance of your work. If you are reading this, we already know something about *you*—in that you are intellectually curious and care deeply about your learners and teaching practices. Our goal is to share ways for educators to be more effective that we have learned, through over twenty years (each!) of teaching practice in PK–12 schools and higher education, and shaped by knowledge of the learning sciences. As teacher educators, we have also learned so much from our bright, collaborative, and dedicated learners—teachers, school administrators, and educators of all kinds.

A crucial indicator of educators' potential for success is teacher beliefs, specifically, the degree to which you believe you can be successful at the task at hand (self-efficacy). Having taught many teachers about how knowledge from the learning sciences can be helpful, we know that at this point, you may be curious but skeptical. We invite you to have some faith that you can accomplish your learning outcomes in studying this content area. Our goal for you is to embrace the idea that small, but powerful changes in your teaching can yield huge impact. Is this book for you? If you are curious, caring, and a little adventurous, yes! We believe in you and your abilities to improve your instructional practices through the learning sciences and digital technologies—like *every* one of our teacher learners.

What Are the Learning Sciences?

The learning sciences are an interdisciplinary area of study comprised of a number of academic fields and the intersections or spaces between them. Among these fields of study are cognitive sciences, educational research, neuroscience, sociology, human-computer interaction, instructional technologies, linguistics, and psychology. The core principle uniting the study of these areas is an interest in the processes of individuals learning alone or in groups. Learning scientists study *learning* and also engage in the design and implementation of effective learning innovations and improvement of instructional methodologies.

In traditional research on education and its systems, processes, outcomes, and phenomena of interest tend to be studied in isolation. In educational research, an important goal of some studies is to determine a *causal* link, that is, a reasonable conclusion that a factor(s) is the cause of an effect and therefore the results are unlikely to occur by chance—they are statistically significant results. This is different from identifying an *associative* link, that is, when things tend to happen together with some reliability. A causal link is an attempt to provide evidence to a predetermined level of confidence or certainty that x happens because of, occurs in the presence of, or affects y and, in order to establish this link, the phenomena tend to be isolated. In contrast, when two or more things occur at the same time with some degree of reliability, they can be described as correlating or having an associative link.

Interest in the new study of learning—which developed into the field of the learning sciences—began in earnest in the 1990s with educational researchers who wanted to look more closely at learning in authentic contexts. Researchers realized the disconnect between outcomes in the classroom and research outcomes in lab settings. They began to try to bridge the gap between research and practice in different ways. An early pioneer of this work, Dr. Ann Brown, described her research as a design science "devoted to the study of learning in the blooming, buzzing confusion of inner-city classrooms," which she investigated by conducting "design experiments" (1992, p. 141). At the time, this was a radical idea—true research happened in controlled environments—not in classrooms!

Modern Teaching and Learning

Your experienced colleagues create the illusion that teaching and learning are relatively easy endeavors. They talk about their "kids" with warmth and enthusiasm, seeming to intuitively understand when certain students are having a bad day, how to reach reluctant learners, and how to challenge their students in just the right ways to engage them in learning. As novice teachers gain experience, they gain expertise. Educational researchers seek to unlock the mysteries of why—and how—some teachers' strategies or approaches are more successful than others. Often, however, a disconnect exists between the findings of educational research and teacher practice in the classroom—particularly in replicating the research results, which may only apply to specific contexts and kinds of learners.

We are at an exciting and revolutionary time in the study of teaching and learning. Information and communication technologies (ICT) and digital technologies have transformed the lives of the PK–12 students we teach, as well as the contexts in which we teach. A paradigm shift has been slowly transitioning the world of education, from a predominant focus on teaching methods and strategies to the consideration of learners' individual differences. Our vocabulary as educators has expanded, including terms such as *connected learning*, *personalized learning*, and *blended learning*. We now focus on using educational technologies for opportunities to create, communicate, collaborate, and think critically. Our ideas of teaching and learning have always been reciprocal in nature; I teach, and my learners learn. The focus has been on the educator building expertise to teach effectively, and how to assess the outcomes of teaching.

In this book, we consider teaching and learning from a different perspective, one that has been slowly gaining momentum in the past two or three decades. In terms of educational paradigm shifts, it's still very new but is rapidly changing our work as educators—the idea that our focus should be on *learning* and not *teaching*. It's a straightforward concept, but becomes profound—like a light switching on—when you realize that teaching and learning are not reciprocal processes. There's no one way to get through to groups of learners because of the infinite complexity of the task to educate others when their prior knowledge—and a myriad of other factors such as motivation, culture, mindset, and language—are different for every single learner! The idea of studying learning processes and the learner through the learning sciences, however, can provide powerful insight by making explicit the principles from which educators can benefit.

Why Learning Sciences, Why Now?

In a complex world, where the outcomes of education are changing locally, nationally, and globally, there is no "secret sauce" for identifying successful teaching practices that work for every learner in every circumstance. More than ever, learning happens *everywhere* and has prompted a shift in emphasis from teacher-centric professional practices to the experiences and outcomes of learners. The interdisciplinary field of the learning sciences, originated by researchers in collaboration with practitioner-researchers (educators who research their practice), is a response to the need to understand how learners learn versus how teachers teach. Learning sciences is an umbrella term, that is, a term which includes a wide range of fields—and that's appropriate, considering the complex and holistic nature of learning itself. Learning scientists study the impact of individual differences, culture, cognition, and context upon learning. They seek to understand the processes of learning for both for individuals and groups. They include educators, cognitive scientists, psychologists, instructional designers, sociologists, educational researchers, linguists, and others incorporating a multidisciplinary approach to learning. By investigating the learning sciences and exploring effective and innovative design for learning with educational technologies, educators can effectively engage learners with digital tools and resources.

> *Learning scientists study the impact of individual differences, culture, cognition, and context upon learning.*

Researchers in learning sciences trial instructional strategies and technologies that can revolutionize educational systems. By combining design thinking methodology with robust theoretical frameworks in the learning sciences, we can improve learning to keep today's youth competitive in the 21st century. This book explores topics such as learning in the digital age, educators as learning designers, and using digital media, tools, and environments, as well as studying practice and impact. These topics have relevance to all stakeholders in education, from educators and educational leaders to policymakers and parents (Figure 0.1).

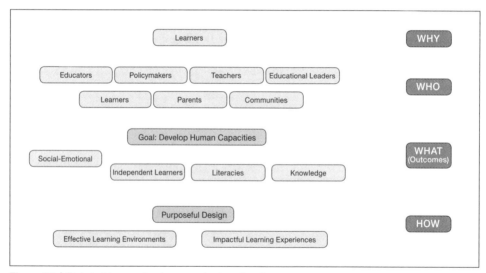

Figure 0.1 | Stakeholders and outcomes of educational processes.

Furthermore, with the interest and need for evidence-based practice, the learning sciences have something to offer each educator. Findings from the learning sciences can provide insight into to instructional problems of practice and present a framework through which to investigate interventions. For example, for a learner desperately struggling with key concepts, it makes a world of difference if an educator is able to test an educated guess that the content is beyond the learner's *zone of proximal development (ZPD)*. Through targeted formative assessment, a more appropriate level of instruction can transform a learner from reluctant and frustrated to motivated and successful. Knowledge of learning sciences findings can provide a framework for tools and practical methods for design experiments—on a variety of scales—to deconstruct and investigate instructional quandaries.

While the idea of the learning sciences may seem unfamiliar and complex initially, consider the years of education, study, and practice that have led to your current experience as an educator. Some ideas you've tried are more successful than others and in your instructional experiments, you've discerned a lot of information in small chunks, based upon trial and error (or *iterations*) as well as through discussions with mentors, coaches, and peers. Instructional problems of practice can be complex problems, but the solutions may be relatively simple, particularly when educators have an understanding of the causes and factors impacting the situation. This requires a kind of practical or *applied* science from which we can understand basic principles and possible solutions. Expert teachers have internalized many such principles—and may even have trouble articulating exactly their thought processes in approaching quandaries in the classroom.

These principles can be more accessible to us all through the practices, research, and approach of the learning sciences. As the expectations from teachers—and their classrooms—become more complex, educators need to be able to have a toolkit of problem-solving routines, and strategies (which could also be considered *algorithms* or *heuristics*) for instructional problems.

These ideas are gaining traction in the world of education, as evidenced by growing interest over the past twenty years. Among several other high profile organizations, the Center for Educational Research and Innovation (CERI), part of the Organisation for Economic Co-operation and Development (OECD) has been studying the brain and learning (bit.ly/2EaAhQd). Harvard Graduate School of Education has championed ideas of the mind, brain, and education (bit.ly/2LUxJfk), and more recently, the Digital Promise organization has shared its work in the learning sciences (digitalpromise.org/initiative/learning-sciences). The International Society for Technology in Education (ISTE), by introducing international standards that mandate the use of findings of the learning sciences in education, has introduced these ideas to educators and leaders working with learners and digital technologies (iste.org/standards).

Course of Mind is ISTE's learning science initiative that aims to empower educators with evidence-based practices grounded in the learning sciences. When educators know and understand the why and how of teaching and learning, the educational landscape—from classroom practice to edtech procurement—is transformed. Course of Mind works to make learning more effective and teaching more efficient with an online course as well as stories and interviews from the field in blog posts, podcast series, and district case-studies. Join in on the learning by following **@courseofmind** on Twitter and visiting the website (courseofmind.org).

Purpose and Scope of This Book

We are teachers first. We love teaching—engaging in the practice of designing impactful and empowering learning contexts for our students. We are also learners. An important element of our practice is trying to convey actionable knowledge to our teacher-learners that will make a difference to their students, and this includes understanding the impact of their teaching upon learners. Chances are that you have very similar goals (educators are passionate about empowering others!).

We are also researchers, learning scientists who consider teaching a design science—and with intentional goals, you can be, too! Any educator can—and should—engage in using evidence-based practices and learn to understand the impact of or modifications needed in design to help reach every learner. In addition to sharing ideas of how you might accomplish this, we share the applicable research in an accessible format that bridges research and practice. We want you to be successful—for you, and for your students!

The field of learning sciences and the application of design sciences to leverage instructional technologies for learner outcomes is vast. Learning scientists explore a range of topics impacting learning. For example, Immordino-Yang and Damasio's study on a topic reasonably familiar to educators—the interconnections between learning and emotions—concludes that "new neurobiological evidence regarding the fundamental role of emotion in cognition holds the potential for important innovations in the science of learning and the practice of teaching" (2007, p. 9). Applied learning sciences can also contribute to the design of instructional tools and materials, for example Lieberman, Fish, and Biely's research on young children's (3–6 years of age) games through the use of eye-tracking systems, and fMRI's (functional magnetic resonance imaging) shows brain activity and emotional responses (2009).

While the field of the learning sciences can be very complex, this book is written for our colleagues in the field to be used as a guide, design toolkit, and source of inspiration. It should be considered an introductory text in this sense. We were inspired to write this book through interactions with our educator-learners, who developed new confidence, expertise, and self-efficacy through understanding and leveraging teaching practices informed by findings from the learning sciences.

These educator-learners were inspired, and we hope to inspire you, too! At the beginning of their learning journeys, teachers are generally unfamiliar with, or had misconceptions about, the learning sciences. We know because we asked them! At the end of the course, however, learners unanimously responded that the learning sciences are very important or essential for practicing teachers.

The main focus of this book is to provide an overview of how previously discon-nected theories and principles can be connected to the outcomes of learning through the study of the learning sciences, and how these principles can be applied to teaching contexts through the application of purposeful design. Our goal is to help you understand individual learner differences and the impact of context upon learning so that you can design powerful learning experiences, particularly when using digital technologies. We will start by taking a look at how the nature of knowing, and consequently teaching of knowledge, is changing and increasing in complexity in the digital age.

How Can the Learning Sciences Help?

Understanding and deconstructing the learning sciences is crucial for 21st century educators. It is critical to know how people learn and the impact of cognitive, social, and cultural factors; how new methods of research are being developed to better serve teachers and students; and how we can transform practices by applying design science. The learning sciences can provide insight into core questions for educators such as:

- How do people learn?

- How do teaching practices impact learning?

- How and when do learner differences matter?

- How can educators study their own (or others') teaching practices for continuous improvement?

- How can educators transform learner outcomes using design informed by learning sciences findings?

- How can educators leverage digital tools for effective learning?
- How can learners be taught to be self-directed and self-monitoring?

Educators may be surprised to find that advances in fields such as educational neurosciences confirm many of the tenets they hold most dear, such as a need to consider students' emotions and physical well-being and the importance of relationships in learning. Conversely, educators may be confused and forced to question their assumptions when discovering deeply-held beliefs about teaching and learning which have been pervasive in education, such as the idea of student learning styles, have been discredited due to lack of evidence. Misconceptions about the nature and processes of learning often seem to be based upon findings from educational research, but upon further examination, the research findings may have been taken out of context or misapplied beyond the scope of the study. Such misconceptions are known as *neuromyths* (OECD, 2007). We will investigate neuromyths common in education—and popular belief—in Chapter 3.

Who Should Read This Book?

This book is written for all educators working in PK–12 environments. Our students are practicing educators who wish to design powerful learning experiences using educational technologies. To do this, they need to understand how learning works.

This book is particularly useful for inservice educators who have some experience teaching and understand the complexity of teaching practice. Although our primary audiences are classroom teachers and teacher leaders, the concepts found in the book are also helpful to instructional coaches, technology integration specialists, media specialists and librarians, and instructional leaders.

How to Move through the Learning Journey

The first years of teaching are quite challenging—there is so much to learn! In the beginning, for novices in teaching or any other profession, thinking and problem solving take time. The situations are unfamiliar and require us to mentally rehearse the possible repercussions of decisions or the reason for learner behaviors. As we gain expertise, our conceptualization of instructional problems changes—as do our ways of thinking about them. For example, driving in a new area of a city is quite a challenge for novices, with so much to observe and pay attention to all while operating a potentially dangerous vehicle. The best way to proceed is slowly. Over time and through experience, a significant portion of driving activities requires less direct attention as they have, in a sense, become automated in our brains and demand less energy or active thinking. As you gain expertise in driving, your thinking about the driving process changes—moving from accomplishing basic processes to more complex considerations, such as how to optimize routes.

Teaching is very similar in that it has a learning curve or trajectory—the things teachers think about, the things they notice, and their questions change over time. Readers will approach the ideas in this book at varying levels, depending upon where they are in the novice to expert trajectory of their teaching experience. This is excellent news because it means that you can read the book again after a year or two of additional practice and interact with the ideas in a different way. In life, we transition between novice and expert states often. While some knowledge or principles transfer to or across different contexts, the ways of thinking may not. For example, as a novice teacher, you learned a great deal about how to work within your subject or grade level, perhaps over several years, gaining expertise. When you move to another subject or grade level, some of your prior knowledge is usable in the new context, but in a sense, you approach it from a novice state once again.

Note to the Reader

Every profession develops its own language which practitioners use when communicating with others in the same field of work. In their communities of practice, practitioners often use specialized language and sometimes this means that we are talking about the same concept—but naming or describing it differently. Professional languages help to define the culture within communities of practice and can be, unintentionally, very intimidating for those new to the field. It can be interesting and helpful to negotiate around ideas during the course of a friendly conversation. That's our goal in this text, to present concepts, viewpoints, and terminologies from different but related fields within the learning sciences, and to help you understand new concepts by building upon your current areas of strength and practices.

How Is This Book Organized?

This book is organized into two parts. In Part 1, we discuss learning theories with a pragmatic approach to understanding how they inform our practices in the classroom or teaching context. We examine learner differences, theories of learning, instructional design, instructional practices, and the design process through the LITE framework, developed by author Angela Elkordy. In Part 2, we share examples and apply the instructional design process to promote knowledge and skills development in the critical areas of the 4C's—creativity, communication, collaboration, and critical thinking.

Special Features

This book includes several features to help you on your learning journey:

ISTE Standards Connection

The ISTE Standards encourage educators and educational leaders to become informed practitioners who thoughtfully incorporate the findings of the field of the learning sciences. Chapters are accompanied by the related ISTE Standards that can be explored to further inform practice. Learn more at iste.org/standards.

Suggested Activities

These easy-to-implement instructional activities are designed for you to try out new ideas to facilitate and enhance your own understanding.

Thinking Like a Designer

Here you are presented with classroom scenarios and asked to reflect on how the reported learning experiences could be designed for more impact. You'll exercise your new knowledge in analyzing instructional problems and proposing solutions based upon design principles. You may consider the scenarios micro case studies of teachers enacting practice.

Fieldwork

These activities are designed to reinforce concepts discussed in the text, with the goal of helping you better understand your own learners.

Learn More

These resources were selected to provide additional, readily accessible information and practical ways to integrate findings from the learning sciences into your own teaching practice. Deep Dive resources provide a more in-depth, theoretically based explanation of concepts for deeper knowledge of a topic.

For additional resources, visit the authors' website: designedlearning.space/design-ed-resources.

PART I

Lessons from the Field: Learning, Design, and Technology

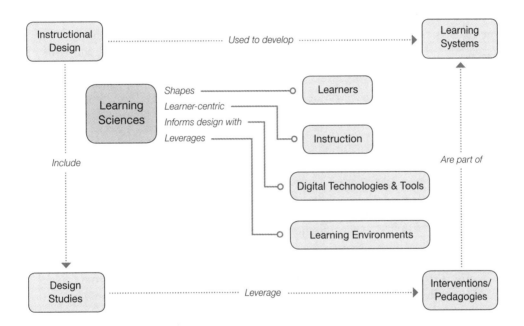

THIS SECTION:

- familiarizes the reader with the field of learning sciences and the role of theories of learning to understand and inform design of digital learning activities and environments

- introduces the unique characteristics of learning in the digital age (including formal and informal contexts)

- identifies and investigates the underlying principles of how learning happens and addresses key questions from a variety of disciplines (for example, cognition and social/emotional factors, human development, and socio-cultural context)

How can we effectively design the instructional environment and digital learning activities in order to make an impact on student learning? How do we know our methods are effective? Educators are increasingly looking to the learning sciences to help them answer these questions. The learning sciences is a rapidly growing field with a recurring theme—theory and practice informing each other in order to design more effective learner outcomes.

Teaching can be considered a *design science* in that good instruction requires educators to think about learning as a system. Within the system, there are guiding principles and interactions between learners, the learning content, instructional methods, materials and tools, teacher-facilitators, and learner-peers. Through repeated iterations or cycles, analysis of outcomes, and modifications to subsequent cycles, the effectiveness of instruction and learner outcomes can be improved.

In Part 1, we introduce the unique characteristics of learners and learning in the digital age in both formal and informal contexts. We discuss the importance of learning theories and contributions from educational research in the learning sciences for impactful teaching practices as well as the purposeful design of learning experiences for targeted learning outcomes. Throughout, we will examine, critique and investigate underlying principles of how learners learn and address key questions from a variety of disciplines and perspectives related to the learning sciences. Our focus is primarily on cognition and social/emotional factors, human development, and design for learning in sociocultural contexts.

We will examine the relationships between learners and learning, teachers and teaching as well as learning environments and the digital technologies and tools used for instruction. In analyzing and then applying these concepts, you'll be developing your practice in line with the vision of the ISTE standards for coaches, educational leaders—and especially, educators. In the ISTE standards framework, educators are learners, designers, facilitators and analysts of teaching and learning.

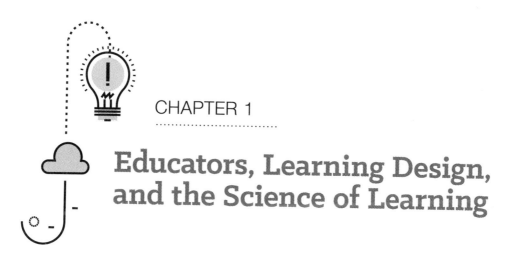

CHAPTER 1

Educators, Learning Design, and the Science of Learning

Teaching is not rocket science; it is much, much harder than that.
—LAURILLARD, 2012, P. 3

Teaching and learning have fundamentally changed in the digital age. Teachers have seen major changes in their roles and the expectations for learners. Digital tools and technologies play a bigger part in education every year. Alongside these changes has been a proliferation of research in the learning sciences that educators can parse, evaluate, and fold into their pedagogy to improve student learning.

In this chapter, we examine how teaching has changed in the digital age, and present general concepts of the learning sciences. We introduce the ideas of learning systems, instructional design, and teaching as a design science.

By the end of this chapter, you will be able to:

- Understand the need to study teaching and learning in different systems, and contexts, both formal (such as classroom settings) and informal (such as libraries and museums), in the digital age.

- Explain the development of, and a rationale for the learning sciences as an interdisciplinary area of study with intertwined bodies of knowledge in several fields.

- Provide a rationale for communities of practice (COPs) for professional learning.

- Explain the conceptualization of teaching as a design science.

- Understand design-based research (DBR) and educational research methodology.

- Understand the LITE framework as a guide for designing experiences which are informed by findings in the learning sciences.

ISTE Standards Connection

The following ISTE Standards are addressed in this chapter:

ISTE Standards for Educators

1. Learner. Educators continually improve their practice by learning from and with others and exploring proven and promising practices that leverage technology to improve student learning. Educators:

a. Set professional learning goals to explore and apply pedagogical approaches made possible by technology and reflect on their effectiveness.

b. Pursue professional interests by creating and actively participating in local and global learning networks.

c. Stay current with research that supports improved student learning outcomes, including findings from the learning sciences.

ISTE Standards for Education Leaders

Connected Learner 5a. Leaders set goals to remain current on emerging technologies for learning, innovations in pedagogy and advancements in the learning sciences.

Why am I only learning about the learning sciences
in my graduate courses and not as an undergraduate?

—GRADUATE LEARNER, WINTER, 2017

Leading Learning in the Digital Age

The proliferation of information, media, and social communications in the digital age compound the complexity of instructional practice. Not only are the tools and strategies for learning significantly different from the recent past (only 20 years ago!), but learner outcomes have also evolved dramatically. For example, it's no longer enough for schools to simply teach factual knowledge. Communities, families, and the students themselves now expect schools to help learners develop the skills, knowledge, and dispositions necessary to engage with and be productive in a globally-networked, digitally-mediated environment. These new expectations and outcomes are entirely different from those deemed essential for success in the past. In his book, *The Social Neuroscience of Education*, professor of psychology Louis Cozolino (2013) describes the mismatch between old-style education and the knowledge and skills needed for today's workplace:

> [M]ost schools are based on a model of industrial production where uniform materials are converted into a predetermined product. This model has proven itself over the last 150 years and works exceptionally well for making automobiles, washing machines, and chicken nuggets. (p. x–vi)

Along with new expectations for learners, there have been dramatic changes in the way in which knowledge is defined, acquired, conferred, and used. Educators are preparing learners for an unknown future where the only certainty seems to be the continuing trajectory of change. The challenges we face as educators are often contextually-bound and complex—with increasingly diversity in our learners, who have a variety of different needs, prior knowledge, languages, and cultural backgrounds.

A recurring theme for educators who are preparing K–20 learners for a new, digitally-mediated, global society is an increased need to understand how people learn, with an emphasis on seeing it from a holistic or systems perspective. This means understanding how cognitive and social-emotional (affective) factors, and sociocultural contexts influence learner differences, as well as how digital technologies interact with these factors and contexts. For example, today's educators are encouraged to see not only the intellectual life of the child but also to be mindful of each individual's unique qualities, such as empathy and leadership. Educators are increasingly called to teach thinking skills, such as how to critically evaluate and creatively solve problems by productively communicating and collaborating with others in technologically-mediated contexts.

The influential Partnership for 21st Century Learning (P21, now a network of Battelle for Kids) framework is widely used in educational contexts as a guide to important 21st century knowledge and skills for learners. The P21 identified the "Four C's" of learning and innovation: critical thinking, communication, collaboration, and creativity. Frameworks for 21st century learning and other resources can be found by scanning the QR code or visiting tiny.cc/79h27y.

Understanding attributes of learners and learning contexts, as well as how they interact, is the work of both educational research and instructional practice. The growing field of the learning sciences—with its origins in areas such as cognitive science, educational psychology, sociology, anthropology, educational research, and more—is a productive ally in the rapidly changing educational landscape. By understanding teaching as a design science, which builds upon and extends educator practice, we can extrapolate and apply principles to design effective learning experiences.

Changing Role of Teachers as Facilitators of Learning

In the digital age, teachers must not only convey information but empower learners to access, process, and create in purposeful, self-directed ways. Today's learners are bombarded with information, often from inaccurate or misleading sources and sometimes to the point of overload, so being able to discern and leverage meaningful knowledge is critical. The skills our learners need for college and career readiness in the coming decades have evolved from discrete knowledge, skills, and capacities to a set of skills for processing, filtering, structuring, and acting upon information in meaningful ways. Educators must genuinely prepare learners for life-wide and life-long learning, in all contexts. In the classroom and beyond, educators must build learners' capacity for thoughtful engagement of content, both as consumers and producers.

As the outcomes of education have evolved, so have the roles and responsibilities of educators. In this rapidly changing context, core learning outcomes and the goals of educator preparation must include a greater understanding of not only how to educate or teach but also how

> **EDUCATOR SURVEY**
>
> At the end of a recent course, Introduction to the Learning Sciences and Technology (at National Louis University), graduate educator-learners were asked: How helpful is the study of learning sciences for practicing teachers?
>
> Despite the new content and ideas of the course for the educators, 100% agreed that study of the learning sciences is helpful for practicing teachers.

our learners learn. By regarding the processes of effective teaching as both art *and* science, where teacher knowledge increases over time and through practice, it is appropriate to consider teaching as the application of knowledge, skills, and pedagogical practices. It is also valuable to recognize that as educators acquire knowledge and insights about teaching and learning, we must also see our work as *iterative*—that is, continually modifying and adapting through cycles of design and instructional practice.

By understanding design principles and learner characteristics in various learning situations, educators can be more effective and strategic in the complex context of the digital age. Understanding learners, how learning happens individually and in groups, how to design effective learning, and how to implement design-based research of learning interventions are core tenets of the field of learning sciences.

In this role, the learning sciences can be described as *translational research* of sorts, that is, a field which specializes in making the outcomes of pertinent research applicable to practice beyond the normal dissemination routes—which are primarily other researchers through technical reports or articles. Pru Mitchell, (2016) describes the need and goals of translational research, a concept which originated in the medical field:

The challenge beyond doing research is to make it easier for practitioners and policy makers to find, understand, and apply research. Translational research makes engagement with practitioners and the wider community its priority. It seeks to 'translate' research in ways that enable that research to be applied. It also 'closes the circle' by allowing practitioners to provide feedback to researchers based on their experience. (p. 4)

Findings of the learning sciences focus on how educators, working together, can build on one another's strengths to improve learner outcomes. In the next section, we'll look at one of those collaborative mechanisms: communities of practice.

Growing Together: Communities of Practice

Communities of practice (COPs) are informal groups of individuals working in the same profession who exchange information about professional practices. In schools, for example, COPs may coalesce around those who have in common the same grade level or content area (e.g., 5th-grade teachers), academic discipline, teaching assignment (e.g., high school biology teachers), or job function (e.g., school librarians or instructional technologists). COPs can be any size but are characterized by shared professional expectations for student outcomes, mutual trust, and a shared commitment for growing their individual and collective practice. A professional learning community (PLC) is one kind of COP. Consider what comes to mind when you think of healthy COP culture. Perhaps you thought of these components:

- Shared understanding of goals
- Shared understanding of practices
- Shared understanding of how to interact successfully with others in the same field (communication norms)
- Specialized language (e.g., professional academic language such as RTI (Response to Intervention), learning targets, standards-based)
- Understanding that there are practitioners who are new to the field (novices) and that gaining deep professional knowledge (expertise) happens over time with practice

One of the challenges for new teachers is understanding the ideas of culture and acculturation. That is, moving into a professional community of practice is a process that takes time to gain an understanding of the community norms, which includes ways of thinking, doing, interacting, and speaking. An interesting—but confusing—aspect of COPs is the use of language which differs across communities, even for the same word or concept! Each profession has its own nomenclature, special terms, and jargon. For example, to different communities of educators, the idea of *practice* could mean:

1. Doing something repeatedly to reinforce newly learned concepts or skills for individuals (practice for reinforcement)

2. Doing something and receiving targeted, corrective feedback (guided practice)

3. The collective application of professional strategies and pedagogies (teacher practice)

4. A specific strategy designed for a targeted outcome (core instructional practice)

5. Warmup or mock activities (athletic practice or theatrical practice in rehearsals)

The use of language in communities of practice is significant. As professionals joining a COP or learning about a related area of practice, we often lose sight of the fact that we are entering a new culture, which is a process that unfolds over time. As Wenger (2011) states:

> Communities of practice have been around for as long as human beings have learned together. At home, at work, at school, in our hobbies, we all belong to communities of practice, a number of them usually ... In fact, communities of practice are everywhere. They are a familiar experience, so familiar perhaps that it often escapes our attention. Yet when it is given a name and brought into focus, it becomes a perspective that can help us understand our world better. [and] perceive the structures defined by engagement in practice and the informal learning that comes with it. (p. 3)

We hope you will see this text as a way to enter into our community of practice. Our goal is to guide you through learning science concepts—and language—which may initially seem unfamiliar because of the academic or area-specific vocabulary but in fact, may represent concepts your communities of practice think about, just using a different approach, lens, or name. Can you think of some examples of different terms for the same ideas? Be sure to use the glossary at the end of this book to look up terms that are unfamiliar.

ACADEMIC LANGUAGE

It can be challenging to understand the academic language in describing the theories and associated concepts educational researchers use to express their ideas.

- *Theories* describe how something is believed to occur, for example, the constructivist theory of learning.

- A *framework* is a kind of scaffold or underlying structure to guide conceptualization of a topic. For example, an assessment framework articulates the elements, their relationships and how they fit together. An example is a curriculum map showing how major assessments work together to ensure targets or standards are addressed through instruction over a term.

- A *model* is a representation of a process, activity or approach. A flow chart is an example of a visual model.

- *Principles* may be considered as guiding rules or fundamental concepts that usually apply in specific contexts or circumstances, such as instructional design principles or principles of learning.

Educational Research and the Learning Sciences

As defined in the introduction to this book, the learning sciences are an interdisciplinary area of study comprised of a number of academic fields (including but not limited to cognitive science, educational research, neuroscience, sociology, human-computer interaction, instructional technologies, linguistics, and psychology) and the intersections or spaces between them. ISTE characterizes the learning sciences as "an interdisciplinary field bringing together findings—from research into cognitive social and cultural psychology, neuroscience and learning environments, among others—with the goal of implementing learning innovations and improving instructional practice" (ISTE, 2016).

The establishment of the field of learning sciences marks the departure from the methodologies and focus of traditional psychology in understanding thinking and learning.

—CHRIS B. (GRADUATE STUDENT, WINTER 2017)

Minding the Gap between Research and Practice

For a long time there has been a perceived disconnect between the processes, as well as the findings, of traditional kinds of educational research and their use in educator practice. Educational research in the past aligned with a philosophy of isolating phenomena in order to study it—using laboratory-like or controlled sessions to create specific circumstances in which to measure the degree of impact of a limited number of factors or variables. Underlying this scientific method was the premise that studies needed to adhere to rigid, highly controlled methods to reliably measure possible effects, to establish a cause and effect relationship, and to then predict events or outcomes.

Other researchers also realized the disconnect between outcomes in the classroom and research outcomes in lab settings. They began to try to bridge the gap between research and practice using different ways. One way was by using a methodology often called *design-based research* (DBR). The goal of DBR is to study an educational intervention, such as a particular program, curriculum, or set of instructional strategies, to improve its success. An intervention—whether it be quite simple or complex—goes through cycles of study and modifications, and is studied in naturalistic contexts such as a classroom (Barab & Squire, 2004). A key difference between DBR and other educational research methodologies is that in the study of interventions, "researchers manage research processes in collaboration with partic- ipants, design and implement interventions systematically to refine and improve initial designs, and ultimately seek to advance both pragmatic and theoretical aims affecting practice" (Wang & Hannafin, 2005, p. 6). The DBR methodology is iterative and often used for investigating questions in the learning sciences and technology-mediated learning interventions or systems.

Furthermore, for many educators, the findings of educational research have appeared to be mysterious and incomprehensible. Much of this has to do with the differing nomenclature and foci of the diverse communities of practice (educational researchers and educators). The learning sciences, with its design-based research approach, however, seeks to bridge the gap between research and practice by involving educators and real classroom settings.

Essential Questions of the Learning Sciences

There are a number of essential questions addressed by research and knowledge creation in the field of learning sciences that are important for practicing educators. They include:

- What is learning?

- How do people learn?

- How do learner characteristics impact learning?

- How can we form strong learning communities?

- How do processes of learning change in different contexts?

- What is the impact of culture in the classroom?

- How can digital tools and technologies best support educators' instructional goals?

These core questions dovetail neatly with the shift from content- to process-oriented skills in 21st century learning initiatives. They also raise crucial questions about how the learning sciences can guide us in understanding how we might appropriately use digital tools and technologies to promote individual learning during school hours. In the past, researchers may have tended to consider discrete aspects of technology and learning instead of systems where learners interact with multiple tools and each other—for example, the impact of specific digital tools for providing student feedback, eye tracking to determine where (and for how long) the learner looks at digital items on screens, or learner analytics from digital games, such as how many times users repeat a level before moving forward. Learning scientists understand that a multidisciplinary view yields greater insight into understanding outcomes in systems of learning, that is, learning interventions studied in context with the normal interactions of learning environments. ISTE is a leader in this growth in understanding that in order to be useful and actionable knowledge for educators, instructional methods, tools and outcomes, a learning sciences informed approach is more productive than research conducted to isolated effects. Recent revisions in the influential and forward thinking ISTE Standards recommend that educators integrate pertinent findings of the learning sciences into their own teaching.

Accessing Educational Research

Educators often feel disconnected from the processes and findings of educational research. That's not surprising, really—just like any other community of practice, educational researchers have their own language, processes, and ways of viewing problems of practice. Any COP has its own language and norms of participation—for example, the language of educators includes all kinds of specialized references, such as standards-based grading, curriculum alignment, Bloom's taxonomy, MTSS (multi-tier systems of support), and Dolch sight words. As experts in their own practice, educators may feel apprehensive about engaging with the research community of practice because of a perceived mysteriousness of the language and practice.

The language and practices of research, however, can be very helpful for educators to identify and understand their own instruction as well as to evaluate impact of instructional decision making. A research methodology adopted by many educators in school settings is known as *action research.*

> Often, action research is a collaborative activity among colleagues searching for solutions to everyday, real problems experienced in schools, or looking for ways to improve instruction and increase student achievement. Rather than dealing with the theoretical, action research allows practitioners to address those concerns that are closest to them, ones over which they can exhibit some influence and make change. (Ferrance, 2000, Introduction)

Action research is carried out by individual educators or teams, working in their own instructional settings. The findings of the research usually result in changes to their practice (or affirm changes are not necessary).

Dr. Elkordy consistently integrates the language and practices of research into her teaching of practicing educators. When educators understand how to measure the effect of their practices and outcomes, they are excited! When educators understand through research and observation how to tweak some of their regular practices—collecting data, observing, reflecting, designing instruction—they become very enthusiastic researchers.

Today, the world is in the midst of an extraordinary outpouring of scientific work on the mind and brain, the processes of thinking and learning, the neural processes that occur during thought and learning, and the development of competence. Over the past decade, there has been a significant increase in the number of publications for practicing educators that share exciting news about how the learning sciences can be relevant to K–20 educators. The Learn More sections in this book share just some of the resources available.

Organizations such as the McREL International (Goodwin, 2018); Digital Promise (the National Center for Research in Advanced Information and Digital Technologies); and the National Academies of Sciences, Engineering, and Medicine (How people learn: II, 2018) have championed a learning sciences-informed approach. In the area of digital tools, technologies and the learning sciences, ISTE is emerging as a leader for practitioner-friendly discussions, ideas, and resources in the learning sciences through the new Course of Mind initiative (courseofmind.org).

Others, such as learning scientist John Hattie and his team, have worked to make vast amounts of educational research actionable by bridging the gap between research and practice. Hattie's original *meta-analysis* (an overall analysis of existing analyses) of the findings of more than 800 educational research papers sought to identify the effectiveness of instructional strategies appearing in the research (2008). Hattie's influential work shares the evidence-based reasoning behind recommended teacher practices. For example, teachers know that teacher-student relationships are critical for student learning but, as a learning scientist, Hattie explains why.

> A primary reason for developing closeness … is to build the trust needed for most learning. Learning requires considerable investment. It requires confidence that we can learn. It requires an openness to new experiences and thinking, and it requires understanding that we may be wrong … learning for many students is a risky business. The positive student-teacher relationship is thus important not so much because this is worthwhile in itself, but it helps to build the trust to make mistakes, to ask for help, to build confidence to try again. (2013, p. 21)

By understanding why the critical role of relationships influences student learning and performance, we can also understand the essential reasons for nurturing these bonds—and why we should lean into them when progress feels particularly tricky. Thinking about your teaching practice and student relationships—do students with whom you have a closer relationship seem to persist to a more considerable degree when you ask them? Learn more about Hattie's key findings by visiting bit.ly/2Vu3sDM.

Figure 1.1 | Japanese Footbridge, by Claude Monet, Image source: simple.wikipedia.org/wiki/Japanese_Footbridge

Teaching as a Design Science

What do we mean when we say design science or applied science? Isn't instruction more an art than a science? To many, art is the expression of emotional beings through creative works whereas science is perceived to be quite the opposite in its measured control and evidence-based nature. The two approaches are often pitted against one another as if there can be no reconciliation. Artist-scientists such as Leonardo da Vinci are touted as exceptions, and this is a point of view which has been sustained over the last two hundred years.

Together, art and science are more impactful, however, than either can be alone. Consider, for example, Impressionist artist Claude Monet. His colorful paintings depict images of the emerging everyday life of turn-of-the-century Paris, the buildings, gardens, landscapes, and portraits seemingly a celebration of modern life in the new Industrial era. For many contemporary observers, Impressionist paintings embodied a rejection of the more severe and scientific Enlightenment era immediately preceding Impressionism.

Monet and his colleagues, however, were the quintessential artist-scientists, because of their design experiments with light and movement. The Impressionists did not paint everyday scenes of Paris or other modern metropolises—they painted the interaction and intersection of *eye–light–object*. They painted the reflected and refracted light radiating and bouncing from objects—a subject matter which demanded a scientific, design-based approach as they endlessly explored the phenomenon of light. The Impressionists built upon the existing knowledge base of materials and subjects, and through a design process, created something new with a different purpose. Famously, Monet painted in series, which were design-experiments in how light changed over time.

In much the same manner, "teaching is a design science in the sense that its aim is to keep improving its practice, in a principled way, building upon the work of others" (Laurillard, p. 8). Almost every teacher has considered: how can I convey the principle of *x* to my learners, or what should my learners be able to do after learning about *y*? When an educator incorporates these professional practices into teaching, they are using elements of an instructional design framework. By understanding the concepts of instructional design, teachers can be more effective designers of learning experiences.

Moving Your Practice to a Paradigm of Design in Teaching

For many of us, lesson planning has been a constant in our practice as educators. While there are similarities between planning and design practices, there are also crucial differences which can constrain or shape learning. Table 1.1 shares these.

Table 1.1 | Comparison of Lesson Planning and Learning Design Practices

	LESSON PLANNING	LEARNING DESIGN
Overarching Goal	Preparedness, activities, resource selection, compliance	Optimizing learning experience for particular learners, in a known environment or space, and with appropriate technologies
Units	Individual lessons or units	Skills or domain level, knowledge and understanding

Continued

	LESSON PLANNING	LEARNING DESIGN
Preparation		
Learners	Teaching to the majority Knowledge aligned with district or building curricula	Majority and individuals by fostering choice and differentiation Aligned with standards more than curriculum, and allows students to bring in their interests
Instruction		
Alignment with Learning Targets or Objectives	For the most part, assume students have appropriate background knowledge.	Elicit prior knowledge to build upon existing knowledge and to uncover misconceptions.
Educational Activities	To engage learners May be isolated or disconnected from the view of the learner	To promote ways of thinking Integrated as part of a continuum
Methods of Assessment	End of chapter or unit tests, standardized testing	Demonstrate level or depth of understanding. Often, competencies aligned with standards.
Reflection	How did the activities go? Are any changes needed in sequence? Classroom management	Includes reflection upon the educational objectives with a mind to improving next iteration Reflects upon the design to understand how learners are learning targeted skills or knowledge Theory of learning informs the next iteration of a design.
Technologies	Focus upon student engagement Emphasis on the consumption of digital media in most contexts No clear understanding of the depth of application of technologies for instruction	How to use the unique affordances or capacities of digital technologies? Emphasis on the creation of learning products A clear understanding of the depth of application of technologies for instruction
Environment	How will this activity fit into a pre-defined space?	Consideration of the ecological factors (or learning system factors) Includes attention to affective factors such as learner emotions, possible anxiety, boredom, etc.

For many teachers, it's not the planning aspect of instruction which is a burden—it's the completion of lesson plans that can seem onerous, particularly for more experienced teachers. Completing lesson planning templates or records is time-consuming, but more importantly, the focus with this method is often on *coverage*—of pages, concepts, or activities. According to a study of lesson planning authoring tools, Sergis and colleagues identified the frequency of commonly occurring elements within lesson plans. Their findings indicated an emphasis on lesson flow, of instructional and assessment activities as well as specific educational objectives in the planning process. This was in contrast to the inclusion of particular assessments, pedagogical approaches, student prior knowledge, or educational problems, which occurred much less frequently (Sergis, Papageorgiou, Zervas, Sampson, & Pelliccione, 2017).

These finding are important in light of trends in design for learning: "A major strand in research into design for learning over recent years has been the development of supportive digital tools that guide teachers' thinking through the process of planning and constructing new learning experience, and revising existing ones" (Masterman, p. 65).

The primary foci of lesson planning are primarily the pace and content to be delivered. The Interstate New Teacher Assessment and Support Consortium (INTASC), however, advocates a different approach in its teacher standards:

> Teachers need to recognize that all learners bring to their learning varying experiences, abilities, talents, and prior learning, as well as language, culture, and family and community values that are assets that can be used to promote their learning. To do this effectively, teachers must have a deeper understanding of their own frames of reference (e.g., culture, gender, language, abilities, ways of knowing), the potential biases in these frames, and their impact on expectations for and relationships with learners and their families (INTASC, 2013, p. 4)

Such an approach places learners at the center of activities and is more compatible with a design-based conception of teaching and instruction, where the learner is the focus, and the process is informed by knowledge gleaned from the learning sciences. We continue our discussion in this chapter, by introducing the LITE framework, and in Chapter 5, in our analysis of design.

Sociocultural Context, Cognition, and Design

Design is a major theme permeating the research and theory of the learning sciences, as are sociocultural context and [learner] cognition. The sociocultural context examines the social, organizational, and cultural structures, dynamics of learning, and teaching situations in classrooms, schools, and beyond. These dynamics may include aspects of culture, language, beliefs, and cultural practices of the learners and their families as well as mediators of these practices such as objects. This contextualization is crucial. According to Elkordy (2016),

> Viewed from a sociocultural lens, processes of learning are highly contextual and are both individual and socially constructed. Learning is embedded and defined within social and cultural frameworks (Vygotskiĭ, 1967; Brown, Collins, & Duguid, 1989; Lave & Wenger, 1991; Bruner, 1996; Wenger, 2000; Lemke, 2001; Brown & Adler, 2008). (p. 29)

Cognition focuses on the construction and organization of knowledge, skills, and understanding as they are acquired—thinking and knowing. *Design* focuses on building environments for learning and teaching, incorporating multimedia, artificial intelligence, computer networks, and innovative curriculum and classroom activity structures. Let's consider each of these as we introduce the LITE framework for learning design.

The LITE Framework: Connecting Learning Sciences to Practice through Design

If we consider teaching as a design science (Laurillard, 2013)—that is, the design of learning experiences within learning systems or environments—we must then define the elements of design—the components of systems. Dr. Angela Elkordy developed the LITE framework use in her teaching of the learning sciences, digital tools, and technologies at the National College of Education (National Louis University). The LITE framework has two interconnected frames or layers. The inner frame (shown in Figure 1.2) encompasses the elements that inform the design process. The four components of the LITE framework are conceived to work together for learning ecologies or systems for *designed* experiences. We intend for the LITE framework to be used as a design tool to prompt consideration and reflection on each element when crafting learning experiences for digital age learning. It is not intended to be a template or lesson plan.

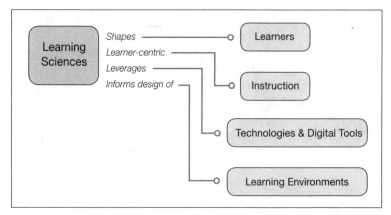

Figure 1.2 | Inner frame of the LITE framework.

The framework prompts educators to consider four big ideas when designing instruction: learners, instruction, technologies and digital tools, and the learning environment. If we think of this in the sense of a learning-sciences informed framework, this means that educators, working as instructional designers, consider the individual differences and capacities of learners, the goals of instruction and pedagogical approach, the effective use of technologies and digital tools, and key aspects of the learning environment. For most educators, these ideas won't necessarily be entirely new. However, using these components as part of a system or a cycle to design learning activities and experiences may shift your paradigm of how learning and teaching work. The following sections share some question prompts to start you thinking about these four big ideas.

Learners

Who are your learners? Which learner characteristics and ways of thinking are important to consider or promote? Consider learner characteristics and actions, particularly learner cognition, emotion, motivation, and prior knowledge. Our goal is to build upon the your existing knowledge base of learner differences. Learner attributes and capacities are discussed in detail in Chapter 3.

Instruction

What kinds of evidence-based instructional strategies are the most impactful for conveying different kinds of content, concepts, and skills? When is it important to understand the science of why strategies work? Or don't work? When looking at instruction, also take into account pedagogical approaches, instructional strategies, and measurements of effectiveness. As you build your teaching repertoire, consider the reasons why some strategies work over others. These ideas are expanded upon in Chapter 4.

Technologies and Digital Tools

What kinds of learning technologies, including non-digital tools, are available? When should we use digital tools and technologies for learning? How can we evaluate their impact? Deciding when and how to use digital tools and technologies from a design perspective is discussed in Chapter 5, and expanded upon in chapters 6 through 9 as we discuss support for learning the 4C's (critical thinking, communication, collaboration, and creativity).

> ### TECHNOLOGIES TAKE TIME TO ADOPT
>
> Every age has its technologies, or tools, to accomplish work. It's not unusual for technologies to take time for adoption, require many iterations, and encounter resistance—particularly in educational contexts. Studies of this phenomenon look at the rate or stages of technology adoption and the rate of innovation diffusion throughout organizations.

Environments

How can we shape the learning environment to be a positive context for learners? What does the idea of *situated cognition* mean for educators? Learning always happens within a context, and as part of a system. Learners bring different goals, motivations, and capacities when interacting with a learning environment. This is also considered in Chapter 5, as socio-cultural context.

We use the inner cluster of the model, the LITE components, to learn about the design parameters or constraints from a learning sciences lens. Who are the learners? What are the instructional goals, methods, and measures? What is the learning context and environment? Considering a broad definition of technologies (from pencils and whiteboards to Chromebooks and robotics), what kinds of technologies would be appropriate to use with these learners for the articulated learning goals within the learning environment? How will you collect evidence of student learning and teaching impact?

The outer portion of the framework (Figure 1.3) shows elements about instructional design and interventions or pedagogies, as well as the study of instructional and learning systems design. This outer layer is important because it shows the day-to-day planning and instruction of classroom educators as well as the deliberate design and measurement of effectiveness as aspects of the learning sciences. Similarly, teaching as a design science requires us to measure or evaluate the evidence—or impact—of teacher behaviors, interventions, and practices for progress towards articulated learning targets or goals.

For example, designing an activity around making would look very different in learning environments depending upon resources—even for the projects at the same grade level. For example, in planning a fourth-grade making project, the instruction, pedagogies, and learners would all be different in environments which are highly resourced, low resourced, or out of school. It is unrealistic to think that all experiences in all learning contexts will be accessible for everyone. In leveraging the

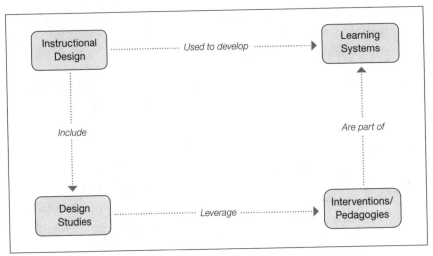

Figure 1.3 | Outer frame of the LITE framework.

learning sciences, our goal is to promote access to crucial skills of developing ideas and ways of thinking. Said differently, while different schools may have different resource levels, they cannot have disparate skill development. This is an equity imperative.

Educators' Conceptions about the Learning Sciences

Circling back to our ideas of the learning sciences area of study, how do educators conceptualize the learning sciences? Here are some initial descriptions of the learning sciences from a diverse range of educators at a recent conference session, in their own words:

- Creating a lens to evaluate learning outcomes through the intersection of cognitive science, pedagogy and technology integration

- Teaching how to observe, analyze, and create meaning

- Methods and reflection that make learning visible

- Methods/styles of learning, outside effects on learning, brain development and learning, "normal" versus exceptional learning, how to best teach for student learning

- Ways of thinking about thinking, learning, and doing

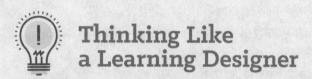

Thinking Like a Learning Designer

Visit to the Art Museum

Georgia and Lexi are 5th-grade teachers. Both took their classes on a field trip to the local art museum to look at Impressionist-era art and then they had their students complete follow-up activities. Afterwards, they discussed their students' experiences.

Georgia shared that she prepared her class for the field trip mainly by reviewing behavior guidelines. She let them enjoy the museum and form their own ideas and opinions about the art. When she asked them what they learned, Georgia's students responded with:

- Art is fun.

- I wish I could paint like the *Starry Night* guy.

Continued

- People must have had a lot of time to draw back then.

- My uncle learned how to paint like that on the internet. It's not hard.

Lexi said that she wanted to use the museum visit as an opportunity to teach her students about science. She prepared a reflective journal sheet, *Is There Science in Art?*, for her students and asked them to work together in pairs to come up with questions about several works of art. The students were directed to look for specific scientific ideas in the art and document them using Google Docs on their mobile devices. Students were asked to share examples of patterns, structure, and function as well as stability and change; all crosscutting concepts from the Next Generation Science Standards. Lexi shared some of the questions her students generated:

- Why are there so many steam engines in the art?

- Why are the paintings purposely fuzzy?

- Why did Monet paint several of the same scenes at different times of the day?

- How can dots of color make a painting?

When they got back to the classroom, Lexi's students wrote a short reflection in their journal blogs to tie all the ideas together. Lexi said that her students were still talking about the visit after two weeks!

Questions for Reflection

- How did Lexi's and Georgia's approaches to the field trip and their classes' learning outcomes differ?

- How did Lexi design with the end in mind?

Chapter Takeaways

- The nature of knowledge and its transmission has changed and with it, teaching objectives and practices for digital learners. The field of the learning sciences provides guidance on how to optimize learning for digital age learners.

- Teaching is complex and educational practitioners should focus on improving practice by understanding the impact of their decisions and actions on student learning. Thinking of teaching as a design science creates a framework for this kind of improvement-oriented analysis.

- Three themes permeate the learning sciences: sociocultural context, cognition, and design. The LITE framework provides a scaffold to consider these themes while designing instruction when using digital technologies or tools.

- Updated theories of learning design are essential to understand in order to keep the learner's experience at the center and use technologies meaningfully to facilitate learning.

Suggested Activities

1. Create a visual representation (such as a graphic organizer, concept map, or other model) of your conception of learning. In it, answer: What is learning to you? How do you think learning works? There are no right or wrong answers.

2. Recall a time when you had a productive learning experience. Describe the experience in 5–10 words which include at least one word for each of the LITE framework elements. For example, if you attended a professional learning opportunity from which you had some great takeaways, your list might look like this:

   - Learner: personalized content, relevant

   - Instruction: small group setting

   - Technologies: collaborative (Google docs)

   - Environment: online, professional learning community

   Now consider a negative learning experience, then describe it in the same manner. Remember, technologies are any tool that helps you accomplish a task, whether that be a pencil, whiteboard, or mobile device. It's only recently that digital technologies have become the prevalent kind of technologies in educational settings. Working with a partner (colleague, friend, spouse), switch descriptions. What are the similarities? Differences?

3. Describe the characteristics of educational research in relation to educator practice. What are your beliefs about and/or experience with educational research? What is the role of research or evidence-based strategies in your practice?

FIELDWORK

Understanding Your Learners

What do you really know about your learners? Have you asked them about their preferences? Their challenges? Understanding your learners in depth is a great way to understand their learning needs. Using a Google form, poll or pencil and paper, create a learning survey to find out more about your students. Questions you might ask (in an age appropriate manner) are:

1. Remember a time when you had a great learning experience. Describe your experience using three words.

2. On a scale of 1–5, with 5 being the most confident, how confident do you feel about mastering x?

3. How do you like to learn when you aren't in school?

4. What would you like me as your teacher to know about you and your learning?

5. How's it going?

Learn More: Resources for Further Exploration

Digital Promise: *Learning Sciences* (digitalpromise.org/initiative/learning-sciences)

Course of Mind: An ISTE initiative (courseofmind.org)

Skills for a changing world: The global movement to prepare students for the 21st century [Video] (youtu.be/pphdxMd5MU0)

Student learning that works: How brain science informs a student learning model [White paper] (mcrel.org/student-learning-that-works-wp)

The Learning Scientists' podcast (learningscientists.org/learning-scientists-podcast)

Edutopia: *Cultivating Student Resilience* by Marilyn Price-Mitchell (edut.to/2WKWGer)

Deep Dive

Hoadley, C., & Van Haneghan, J. (2011). The Learning Sciences: Where they came from and what it means for instructional designers. *Trends and Issues in Instructional Design and Technology* (3rd ed., pp. 53-63). New York: Pearson.

Learning Designer: *The Learning Designer is a tool to help teachers and lecturers design teaching and learning activities and share their learning designs with each other* (www.ucl.ac.uk/learning-designer)

National Academies of Sciences, Engineering, and Medicine. (2018). *How People Learn II: Learners, Contexts, and Cultures.* Washington, DC: The National Academies Press. https://doi.org/10.17226/24783.

Sawyer, R. K. (2008). Optimizing learning implications of learning sciences research. *Innovating to learn, learning to innovate, 45,* 35-98.

CHAPTER 2

Learning in the Digital Age: Theories and Implications

A basic understanding of processes of learning is essential for those who intend to develop activities that will have the potential to lead to effective learning taking place in the classrooms—that is, teachers.

—PRITCHARD, 2018, P. 2

For many of us, theories about learning are what excited us about becoming teachers in the first place. Theories—the accumulated wisdom of educators and scholars over time—helped us see the big picture of the educational landscape as we were entering the profession. But what is the role of theories of learning once we leave the university and become practicing educators? How can educators leverage learning theories in their own practice, especially when there are so many theories from which to choose?

In this chapter, we review the three main theories of how people learn—behaviorism, cognitivism, and constructivism—and their applications in learning contexts. Our focus is on sharing principles and ideas that shed light on why or how some strategies work so that you can better apply them in your instruction. We will show you how to connect these theoretical concepts of how people learn with your daily practice.

This will help you as you design engaging, high quality lessons for all diverse learners.

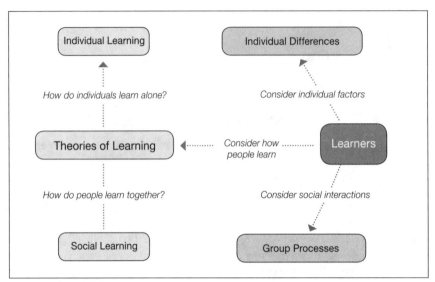

Figure 2.1 | The LITE framework applies theories of learning to consider individual and group learning.

By the end of this chapter, you will be able to:

1.   Articulate a personal conceptualization of learning.

2.   Explain the role and impact of theories of learning in the classroom.

3.   Differentiate among the behaviorist, cognitivist, and constructivist learning theories.

4.   Consider how educators can conceptualized the processes of learning through visual representations.

5.   Analyze the conceptual shift from teacher-centric to learner-centric educational approaches.

ISTE Standards Connection

The following ISTE Standards are addressed in this chapter:

ISTE Standards for Educators

Learner 1a. Set professional learning goals to explore and apply pedagogical approaches made possible by technology and reflect on their effectiveness.

Learner 1c. Stay current with research that supports improved student learning outcomes, including findings from the learning sciences.

Designer 5c. Explore and apply instructional design principles to create innovative digital learning environments that engage and support learning.

Educators, Ideas, and Learning

As educators, we may not regularly consider theories of learning, primarily because the theoretical concepts seem at times to be so far removed from our practice. We do, however, often think deeply about the processes and procedures of teaching. We think about how to present a topic or concepts, the pedagogical approach, the sequence of instructional units through the year as well as how to adjust our timing for testing, holidays and family/community events. We may consider the prior knowledge, in terms of content knowledge and skills, required to understand the material, and plan exciting activities to engage our students around the ideas. Then, we think about how to best differentiate the material for our English language and other diverse learners in our classrooms. On the commute back home from work, in the teachers' lounge, or while grocery shopping, we deconstruct our teaching practices as we reflect on how well the lesson went and imagine improvements for the next time. The degree of student learning, for many teachers, is secondary to the teaching practice. This is not a value judgment about importance or priority, but more of a focus upon quality teaching. As we reflect, the implicit assumption is that teaching practice leads to students' learning. The two ideas seem inextricably linked—teaching and learning go together.

When we ask our teacher candidates about learning, they usually describe it in terms of teaching practices and the things educators do, such as hands-on learning, direct instruction, visual learning, or personalized learning. With the pressure to move forward with curriculum and keep up with scope and sequence, our focus—particularly for novice and intermediate teachers—is content and how we are going to cover the curricular requirements. Student learning outcomes are often measured by unit or end-of-chapter tests in the classroom or by reviewing standardized test results in grade level teams.

In this chapter, we will show you how to connect theoretical concepts of how people learn with your daily practice. Our focus is on sharing principles and ideas that shed light on why or how some strategies work, and in doing so, empower your teaching.

How do we know our students are learning meaningful knowledge and skills? At first glance, the answer seems rather obvious—because we are teaching them, of course! But what do we learn from assessments or tests? When using unit tests for measurement, most teachers know that there isn't time to go back and talk about material students didn't understand, particularly when there is pressure to maintain a prescriptive pace of content coverage. When we reflect upon summative assessments, such as standardized tests or end-of-unit tests, the information we consider is primarily to inform us about how successful the curriculum and instruction have been and point us to potential adjustments needed when teaching next time. This kind of assessment, that is, assessment of learning (summative) is quite different from assessment for learning (formative), where the goal is to see students' current understanding so that we can provide adjustments in real time to guide subsequent learning.

Truly understanding how learning works can be transformative to your teaching practices, helping you to maximize learning outcomes despite limited time and multiple curriculum objectives. This is why educational psychology and cognitive science are at the core of the field of the learning sciences. Understanding how to assess the outcomes of your teaching and measure the impact on student learning—not just at test time but throughout the teaching day—requires an understanding of how people learn, how to effectively—and precisely—measure learning against target objectives, and how to leverage instructional practices to meet learners' needs. First, however, it is necessary to understand the idea of learning. What exactly is it?

Teaching and Knowledge Transmission

Teaching and learning are ancient practices that define us as human beings. We are wired to be social learners, to exchange information and interact with others. In an apprenticeship model, parents and elders taught skills to the next generation, who had guided practice in hunting, gathering, communicating, and parenting followed by gradual release to pursue the skills on their own. Professor of Cognitive Neuroscience at the University College of London, Sarah-Jayne Blakemore, and colleagues consider:

> [T]he human brain becomes tuned to processing social information, thus paving the way to benefit from others' knowledge and instruction. This has important implications for education because it demonstrates that the fundamental social capacities, which facilitate and profit from teaching and instruction, are laid down early in development. In fact, it has been proposed that social communication among humans is adapted to facilitate the transmission of generalizable knowledge between individuals. This communication system has been termed "natural pedagogy," and is thought to enable fast and efficient social learning of cultural knowledge. (Blakemore, Grossmann, Cohen-Kadosh, Sebastian, & Johnson, 2013)

In the beginnings of formal education, teaching was relatively simple, and the means of knowledge acquisition and transmission were reasonably predictable, involving direct contact with knowledgeable others—teachers. Students learned directly from intensive questioning by their teachers or mentors in *Socratic circles*, developed in Ancient Greece by their namesake Socrates, a method still used today. Lectures were replicated through memorization and very few texts—reproduced by hand—were available. During the Middle Ages and the Renaissance, apprentices and learners worked with masters to gain understanding and were supervised, mentored, and provided with guided practice to develop expertise.

Teachers and masters directly shared their own expertise, which was gained chiefly from their experience and learning. Because of this, the transmission of knowledge was limited by physcial distance. Information and ideas spread slowly, leaving a traceable path of influence; for example, along the Silk Road trading route, "the constant movement and mixing of populations also brought about the transmission of knowledge, ideas, cultures and beliefs, which had a profound impact on the history and civilizations" (UNESCO, n.d.).

As the practice of writing developed, students bore responsibility for comprehending, synthesizing, and using new skills and concepts. Opportunities for sharing of knowledge beyond larger cities on trade routes, that is, the realm of person to person transmission, also changed. Writing and the ability to read became valuable societal differentiators because they allowed knowledge to be spread not only orally but across great distance while maintaining the essence of the originator's story. With the development of the printing press and the ability to replicate large amounts of the same content, the dispersal of knowledge was much more widespread. Teachers used their perceptions of others' ideas as shared through print media to share expertise and gradually, their students were able to read themselves.

MENTAL MODELS

When we ask our educator-learners to think about what is learning, there is an interesting array of answers. Their conceptualization of learning varies depending on their ideas about their own practice. It's important to note that our *mental models*—the way we conceptualize or think about a topic or thing—in many ways frame our understanding and approach to solving instructional problems of practice. Instructional coach Elena Aguilar explains:

> Mental models are our values, beliefs, and a series of assumptions about how the world works. Unconsciously, we create a story about other people, institutions, and the world which drives our behavior. While everyone has them (in fact, we need them to make sense of the complex world in which we live), all mental models are flawed to some extent and usually invisible to us. (2015)

Our mental models are shaped by our beliefs and change the way we actually see and respond the world. This includes our ideas about learning; as we will see in Chapter 3, many teachers believe that students can learn better in different modes (auditory, visual, and kinesthetic). This mental model has garnered a great following in the teaching field, but in fact, is not supported by research evidence and has been discredited as a myth (Riener & Willingham, 2010).

In an oral culture, knowledge is limited to direct or indirect experience, mediated by both an orator's abilities to relay the information, and upon recipients' ability to fully comprehend. Furthermore, to acquire new information, access to a knowledgeable individual is necessary, and a limiting factor. In contrast, the advent of writing and the printing press meant that ideas could spread through written materials and books.

For educators, who usually lived and worked within small geographical ranges with few shifts in population, this meant that it could be possible to have a good understanding of learners' prior knowledge and worldview. Teaching was less complex in terms of (acknowledged) differences among learners. With the advent of the digital age and the exponential increase in both the development and dissemination of information, however, it's impossible to know the sources or extent of learners' prior knowledge. This adds to the complexity of teaching. Learners' prior knowledge is also impacted by motivation, engagement, type of feedback received, and learning environment. Instructional strategies and supports are also examples of variables in teaching ecologies and systems of learning.

What Is Learning?

Before we can show evidence that learning has occurred, we need to understand what it actually is and how it happens. While there are many definitions of learning, almost all descriptions contain the idea that learning is a change that happens as a result of interaction with ideas, things, or people. The prevailing view among contemporary educational theorists is that people construct their own knowledge based on their previous knowledge and their understanding of where new knowledge fits within it (Bransford & Cocking, 2000). Bransford et al. contend in the seminal first volume of *How People Learn*:

> A logical extension of the view that new knowledge must be constructed from existing knowledge is that teachers need to pay attention to the incomplete understandings, the false beliefs, and the naive renditions of concepts that learners bring with them to a given subject. Teachers then need to build on these ideas in ways that help each student achieve a more mature understanding. If students' initial ideas and beliefs are ignored, the understandings that they develop can be very different from what the teacher intends. (2000, p. 10).

It is essential for educators to understand the way in which knowledge is constructed and the crucial importance—and quality—of prior knowledge. Teachers, however, have vastly different ideas of how learning happens, based upon their knowledge gained in teacher preparation programs, their experiences in the classroom, and their beliefs as well as their misconceptions or misunderstandings, some of which may have originated from well-meaning but ill-informed sources. In his white paper, *Student Learning That Works: How Brain Science Informs a Student Learning Model*, researcher Bryan Goodwin commented upon this anomaly:

> [I]f you were to ask 100 teachers how learning works, [i]t's doubtful you'd hear much clarity, specificity or uniformity in the answers. Let that soak in for a moment. Something as critical to learning as how it actually works

is seldom articulated or acted upon by education professionals when designing or discussing teaching strategies or addressing student learning difficulties. (2018, p. 1)

It's little wonder that educators have such a wide range of responses because until now, how learning occurs hasn't been much of a focus of teacher preparation programs or professional development; rather the emphasis has been on deepening expertise in teaching. Findings from the learning sciences can help inform this view for greater understanding. Also, there is a wide range of methodologies and approaches to support teachers in forming research-based opinions, through action or design-based research, about how learning works with their own learners in learning systems.

Theoretical Frameworks

For hundreds of years, cognitive scientists and others have been trying to understand and articulate how learning works. Most of them express their ideas in terms of a framework or model. Think of research-based theoretical learning frameworks as educated ideas or hypotheses—with supporting evidence—about how learning works in particular contexts. Another way to view a framework is as a scaffold or skeleton; researchers may have discovered many of the essential points about what works, but you don't necessarily have to see evidence in every boundary or aspect of the frame. A theoretical framework or model created for a particular context can be used as a guide to predict outcomes. The anticipated results are stated as hypotheses, which are then studied for accuracy.

As the idea of knowledge and learning in formal contexts has changed, so has the supporting evidence as well as predicted outcomes of successful practices. For example, for a long time, the model or expectation of learning was to be able to reproduce particular sets of knowledge. A simple model of that transmission of knowledge from an expert to a novice might look like this:

Teacher talks + student listens = student learns

If a teacher uses this as a model and you are troubleshooting an instructional problem, you may immediately consider that the student wasn't listening, and any instructional adjustments would be based upon that premise. But, as experienced educators know, this analysis reflects a very simplistic view of learning. Obviously, a more complex model is necessary to meet today's expectations of learning.

By understanding learners on a deeper level, as Linda Darling-Hammond of Stanford Graduate School of Education emphasizes, teachers are able to extend more personalized opportunities for all diverse learners. She also proposed that a more complex knowledge base is needed, with specialized teacher knowledge beyond instructional strategies and content knowledge, noting: "This understanding of learners and learning, I would argue, is the most neglected aspect of teacher preparation in this country" (1995, p. 13).

We will discuss some more meaningful and specific instructional strategies in Chapter 4, but for now, let's look at theories of learning which shape teaching methods and strategies. For some readers, this content will be new, whereas others may find the content somewhat familiar, having encountered it in preservice preparation. We hope you have new insights!

Theories of Learning: A Brief Overview

Theories of learning can be useful frameworks for understanding the complicated dynamics of teaching and learning. Learning theories help us understand and answer questions about how we learn as well as provide guidance to teachers as they design educational environments and endeavor to create optimal experiences for all learners.

While there are many theories of learning, we can consider the following—and their offshoots (see Figure 2.2)—as most influential in the classroom: behaviorism, constructivism, and cognitivism. The following sections present an overview of each theory with classroom applications. It's important for educators to understand that there are aspects of each theory that can be effectively applied in learning contexts, and because of the complexity of learning, we shouldn't be seeking one theory which applies in all contexts. While an in-depth analysis of learning theories is beyond the scope of this book, we do recommend additional materials for interested readers to explore in the Learn More section at the end of the chapter.

Behaviorism

Behaviorist learning theories are concerned with observable results, taking into account feelings or thoughts and responses to prompts. Watson (1930) defined behaviorism by saying that, behaviorism is the scientific study of human behavior. Its real goal is to provide the basis for predication and control of human beings and control of human beings. Given the situation, to tell what the human being will do: given the man in action, to be able to say why he is reacting in that way. (p. 2)

Watson based his theory of behaviorism on the idea that behaviors are acquired through *classical conditioning*. According to behaviorist learning theory, the most important thing is observable results. The focus is on good grades, good test scores, good results. B.F. Skinner (1938), another behaviorist theorist, introduced the importance of *operant conditioning*, folding the concept of reinforcement into this theory of learning. The focus is on how quickly a behavior is learned and the likelihood that a response will take place.

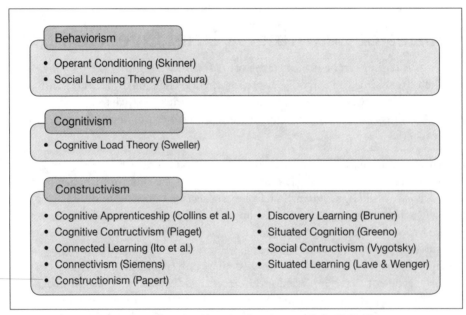

Figure 2.2 | Influential modern educational learning theories and their offshoots.

Some examples and applications of the behaviorist learning theory in the learning environment are rote classroom work, repetitive classroom work and practice, verbal praise as reinforcement ("You did a good job!"), and reward/point classroom management systems.

Not all educators are convinced that classical conditioning, where a student associates a particular response when recognizing a prompt, shouldn't have a role in K–12 education. Teacher Jordan Johnson, writing on the question and answer discussion site Quora, explained the possible consequences—sometimes unintended—and possible uses of this strategy for classroom management:

> I don't agree that operant conditioning has no place in K–12 education or homeschooling. I'd contend that regardless of whether you believe it should happen, it happens on a level that parents and teachers may not be conscious of, because there often are unconsidered adult behaviors that reward or punish the children's behavior (whether the adult intends it or not). Classroom management is all about organizing the class environment, time, and activities to maximize learning and growth. Part of this is establishing a safe and respectful environment with open communication channels, and some procedures play into that. (2015)

TEACHERS THINK: BEHAVIORIST STRATEGIES

The theory of behaviorism centers on the assertion that learning itself is a mechanical process. In practice, the behaviorist approach provides students with a stimulus, designed to provoke a response in the learner. The ideal result of this exposure to the stimulus is a new behavior. If the desired behavior is not demonstrated adequately or at all, the desired behavior is reinforced. The measure of learning in this context is a visible change in the behavior of the learner.

—CHRIS B.

My students have always responded well to rewards and positive reinforcement. Therefore, in the beginning of the semester when I am teaching them to be in their seats when the bell rings and working on their warm up, on day 2 or 3 I used to walk around and give praise and candy to the students doing the right thing. The following day, all students would be in their seats doing what they are supposed to be doing because they all want the reward. I have found the ramification of this is that the reward for doing the right thing is to be expected instead of doing the right thing because it's the right thing to do.

—JAMIE J.

Which behaviorist strategies are you using? What kinds of behaviors (intended or not) are you reinforcing?

In practice, educators use behaviorist strategies mostly for reinforcing positive behaviors or community building, for example, using a token economy or similar reward system, or software such as Class Dojo (classdojo.com) or Edmodo (edmodo.com). Another strategy is acknowledgement of accomplishment of behavioral or academic goals (e.g., using digital badges such as classbadges.com or badgr.com). This kind of interaction can be described as *transactional* and provides *extrinsic motivation* in that students receive external praise or approval for performing in expected ways.

Cognitivism

Behaviorist theories of learning were prevalent in the first half of the twentieth century, but did not consider the impact of internal events such as thoughts, beliefs, or feelings (Schunk, p. 21). These theories seemed to tell only part of the story to theorists who considered the cognitive processes of learners as important, as well as how we think and gain knowledge. Cognitivism can be described as an information processing theory because cognitivist theories of learning view the learner as a processor of information rather than an acquirer of learned behaviors. These theories are focused upon the internal processes—acquiring, encoding, and storing information; thinking; memory; knowing; and problem-solving—that take place during the learning process. In 1980, George Miller founded the Center for Cognitive Studies at Harvard with Jerome Bruner. Both Bruner and Miller are considered to be the major theorists of cognitivism. Bruner (1957) posited that the outcome of cognitive development is thinking. The mind creates from experience "generic coding systems that permit one to go beyond the data to new and possible fruitful predictions" (p. 234). The ability to invent ideas for oneself is an important outcome of cognitivism.

According to Shuell (1986), "information processing theories focus on how people attend to environmental events, encode information to be learned and relate it to knowledge in memory, store new knowledge in memory, and retrieve it as needed." One of the most important ideas in cognitivism is schema theory.

> A schema is a cognitive construct that organizes the elements of information according to the manner with which they will be dealt. An early discussion of schemas was presented by Bartlett (1932). He demonstrated that what is remembered is only partly dependent on the information itself. Newly presented information is altered so that it is congruent with knowledge of the subject matter. Knowledge of subject matter is organized into schemas and it is these schemas that determine how new information is dealt with. (Sweller, 1994, p. 296)

Schemas can be considered a kind of classification system of thought patterns about processes, objects, and ideas—a kind of mental system of categorization that includes information about defining features. The idea of schema highlights the importance of prior knowledge in organizing categories of information and creating relationships or patterns out of bits of information. When misconceptions occur during learning, they can impact future knowledge building. Context can be very important in creating and differentiating schema—consider, for example, the mental image you have of the concept blue. How many schema represent the idea of blue in different contexts?

A particularly important idea for educators which considers the concept of schema is *cognitive load theory*, proposed by Sweller (1994). The premise of cognitive load theory is that the difficulty of tasks—even the same tasks for different leaners—differs in how much they demand cognitively of the learner. A major goal of the brain is to minimize cognitive load by creating automatic processes—which require less mental effort—for frequent sequences of thought. For example, think back on learning to drive. Remember the incredible complexity when you first began and how over time, processes became more automatic?

Sweller also explained how sequences of cognitive processes can be formed into schema:

> In a similar manner, there are schemas for dealing with problems. These schemas allow the classification of problems into categories according to how they will be dealt with, i.e., according to solution mode. (p. 296)

TEACHERS THINK: COGNITIVIST STRATEGIES

Despite being developed as a response to behaviorism, cognitivism still views learning as a very mechanical process. Although no emphasis is placed on structuring behavior and the theory seeks to create active learners, the classroom remains almost entirely teacher-centered. A teacher-centered learning environment remains necessary in this approach due to the need for the students to be presented with information that they can then process and store for later retrieval. While this is a very efficient, organized way in which to structure teaching and learning, and which aims to break complex problems down into more manageable chunks, because of its rigid and mechanical approach, students find difficulty in adapting to unexpected changes.

—CHRIS B.

Saving problem solving strategies as schema—that is, a stored sequence of steps also called *heuristics* or *algorithms*—is one reason why it is critical for learners to build effective problem solving strategies and develop content knowledge for deeper learning and higher-order thinking. When learners are engaged in problem solving, they will quickly do a mental check to recall strategies they've used previously to solve that particular kind of problem. If the type of problem is new or unrecognized, it can be hard to know where to begin—which is where it is helpful to prompt learners (Asking: Why don't you start here? When did you encounter this before?). Problem solving strategies or schema are associated with contexts—the contexts in which they were learned. This is why it is essential for teachers to be explicit in bridging the same kinds of thinking in different contexts, for example, explaining to students that understanding how to divide an 8-portion pizza into equal parts is a fraction problem.

According to Sweller, "Evidence for the importance of schemas comes from work on novice-expert differences that suggests that differential access to a large store of schemas is a critical characteristic of skilled performance" (p. 298). The idea of schema also explains why it is critical to elicit learners' prior knowledge to uncover misconceptions—or to be patient while learners make sense of new information when they have little background in the topic!

The Cognitive Science of Education is an excellent 14-part series written by Peter Nilsson, English teacher and director of research, innovation, and outreach at Deerfield Academy in Massachusetts. This web-based resource on cognitive science is particularly useful for educators. In the second module, Nilsson's diagram (Figure 2.3) lists the elements of the information processing theory.

Briefly, the information processing theory proposes a model whereby a learner extends attention to a sensory input and then decides very quickly if further action is needed on the perception. The information is then passed on to working memory

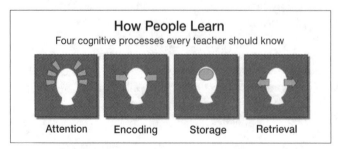

Figure 2.3 | Information Processing theory elements.

for further processing and perhaps being encoded into long term memory or discarded. When information in long-term memory is retrieved, at first, it's usually only in a similar context until the learner (or educator!) makes explicit connections. We'll discuss attention, memory, and processing in greater detail in the following chapters.

Constructivism

This influential theory of learning builds upon aspects of behaviorist and cognitivist theories. It proposes that we actively construct our knowledge based on our unique experiences. A focus of the constructivist theory is the uniqueness of each learner.

According to educational researcher David H. Jonassen,

> The difference between a constructivist view of instructional design and what he calls an objectivist view (behavioural and cognitive) of instructional design is that the objective design has a predetermined outcome and intervenes in the learning process to map a pre-determined concept of reality into the learner's mind, while a constructivist view maintains that because learning outcomes are not always predictable, instruction should foster learning and not control learning (as cited in Ratna & Tron, 2015, [p. 10])

Constructivism has two main theorists. Jean Piaget proposed four stages of cognitive development: the sensorimotor stage (ages 0–2 years), the preoperational stage (2–7), concrete operational stage (7–11), and the formal operational stage (12+). He conceived of learning as an individual activity (Schunk, 2012). Lev Vygotsky, however, believed that the individual constructs their own understanding but within a social context to which it is effectively bound.

Vygotsky developed the term *zone of proximal developmental* (ZPD), which refers to the difference between what a student can do without help, and what a student can do with the help of a more knowledgeable *other*. According to Vygotsky (1986), the teacher takes on the role of the facilitator in the learning environment, tailoring their interactions to each student's ZPD in order to help them master the skill. Dixon-Krauss (1995) discusses teachers' scaffolding of students' knowledge when working with their ZPD and notes that teachers mediate learning through social interactions, maintain flexible roles, and support each student based on individual needs.

Constructivist approaches are considered more student-centric than teacher directed. Examples of constructivism in the classroom environment are inquiry-based research projects, problem-based learning, peer-led discussion groups, and heterogeneous (mixed ability) reading groups.

In adopting an approach through which learning is *doing*—through making, hands-on activities, or experiments—educational technologists follow in the footsteps of Seymour Papert, Piaget's student and an early innovator of computing for learning. Papert endorsed what he called *constructionism*, and advocated for the revolutionary idea of children as computer programmers in 1971! (Papert, 1971)

Educators should expand their knowledge of learning theories to supplement and empower the way they think about learning. By considering the implications of these theories of learning, and our desired outcomes for all our learning experiences, we are better able to create meaningful learning experiences.

"Theory is something that is able to explain what is observed, upon which strategies—what is actually done in the classroom to achieve particular learning outcomes—are based" (Pritchard, 2018, p 4). Theories should provide a basis for what works, why and when—with the important caveat that there is no one-size-fits-all approach or framework. Consider this knowledge as part of a teaching and learning toolkit. Like any new or unfamiliar tool, understanding the purpose, use, and impact takes deliberate practice and experience.

Considering digital learners, tools, and technologies adds an entirely new way of viewing the traditional learning theories and adds exciting new ways explore how learning works. We will describe these theories and implications later in the chapter, but for now, in considering what the role of learning theory and classroom practices is—you should be thinking that as a best case scenario they are informing one another in a key and lock way.

Constructivism recognizes that the context of learning is a crucial element that shouldn't be separated from cognitive processes. Schunk (2012) explains:

> A core premise of constructivism is that cognitive processes (including thinking and learning) are situated (located) in physical and social contexts ... Situated cognition (or situated learning) involves relations between a person and a situation; cognitive processes do not reside solely in one's mind. (Greeno, 1989, p. 233)

Situated cognition or situated learning is a highly influential theory used in instruction and educational psychology and as such it is important for schools and public learning contexts such as museums and libraries. It emphasizes the idea that learning is more meaningful in authentic contexts and applications.

> "Situated" means that knowledge is not just a static mental structure inside the learner's head; instead, knowing is a process that involves the person, the tools and other people in the environment, and the activities in which that knowledge is being applied. (Sawyer, 2008, p. 3)

Situated cognition supports the assertion that teaching is a design science. Selecting and setting the conditions, environment, and materials for learning—for example, the time of day, the curriculum materials and pedagogical approaches, the digital tools and materials, and instructional strategies—all have performance consequences for learners.

TEACHERS THINK: CONSTRUCTIVIST STRATEGIES

Constructivism builds upon the legacy of behaviorism and cognitivism, yet makes a few significant departures from the aforementioned theories. In contrast to both, constructivism aims to develop and measure the knowledge students construct for themselves. To do this, constructivism relies heavily on empowering students to make decisions in their learning experiences, with the goal that allowing students to carve out more meaningful and relevant experiences leads to true development of new knowledge and skills. A major point of emphasis when exploring and implementing a constructivist approach to teaching and learning is the importance of context. By emphasizing the need to situate learning in such a way that students have control of their learning, constructivism moves learning away from an act of pure consumption of information to one that is almost entirely based on the discovery of information and new knowledge.

—CHRIS B.

I consider the zone of proximal development when forming groups in my world language classroom. I find it highly effective to pair students with other students who can understand, use, and explain the information better than they can themselves. It is beneficial to learn from your peers, and I have figured out that students often times can explain it and help each other sometimes more than I can.

—JAMIE J.

Representations of Learning Processes

While we may share some common ideas about how learning works, the way in which we conceptualize this process can differ widely. So how might we best communicate our conceptualizations of learning with one another? A visual representation of a process, concept, or procedure—this can be a graphic organizer or a diagram—can illustrate how an educator conceptualizes the ideas or content. Figures 2.4 and 2.5 share visual representations created by educators when they were asked to share their conceptions of learning.

A concept map has a distinct, different purpose than a visual organizer, in that concepts and the relationships between concepts are articulated by linking phrases between the central ideas or nodules. By using descriptive linking phrases, we can understand the relationships between the concepts. Skillfully created concept maps can reveal the underlying mental models of how people conceptualize or think about ideas. See the concept map at the beginning of Part 1 of this book for an example.

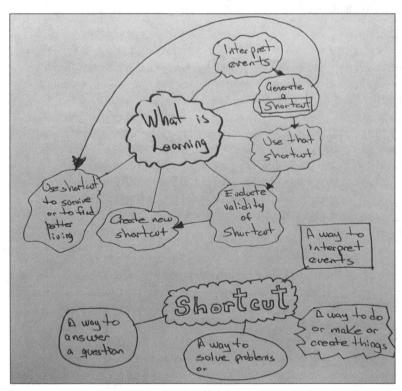

Figure 2.4 | Educator's conception of learning (from authors' ISTE conference presentation, 2018).

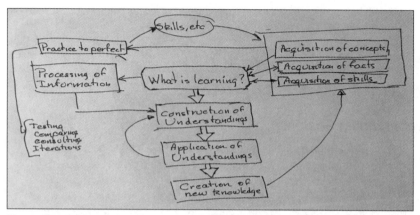

Figure 2.5 | Educator's conception of learning (from authors' ISTE conference presentation, 2018).

In using visual representations, educators can explore how their colleagues conceptualize their ideas—in other words, their mental models. Group discussions around learning can be clarified and enriched when collaborators use concept maps or other kinds of visuals to share their ideas.

Chapter Takeaways

- Evidence-based theories of learning such as behaviorism, cognitivism, and constructivism are important for educators to understand in order to inform design of learning experiences.

- The predominant view of learning is that knowledge is individually constructed through cognitive processes. These frameworks keep the learner's experience at the center.

- From a practical perspective, educators should understand how learning theories support good teaching and learning strategies by providing principles that can be applied to learning design.

- Educators form their own ideas of how learning happens, which may (unintentionally) include misconceptions.

- The trend in learning theories has been to look more deeply at the role of the learner and to understand influences in knowledge building such as culture, context, and prior knowledge.

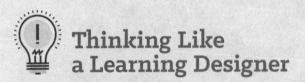

Thinking Like a Learning Designer

Students Helping Students

Sanjay and Sara, two fifth grade teachers, have been working hard to set up groups in their respective math classes. Sanjay's approach is to set up groups of students with homogeneous ability so that he can work with them in small groups together. Sara has set up heterogeneous groups with careful attention to select students with mixed abilities. Both teachers have encouraged students to help one another. You are observing both rooms.

Questions for Reflection
- What do you think you will see?
- Which students do you think will perform better and why?

Suggested Activities

1. As a preservice teacher, you were encouraged to begin to develop your teaching philosophy, which you've probably updated during the course of your career. Now consider your *learning philosophy* and articulate your current beliefs and understanding of learning.

2. Examine your own patterns of learning and extrapolate general principles about when you learn best. For example, certain times of the day might be better for activities such as reading, reflecting, planning, deconstructing, or grading. Track your learning over a day, then a week, and then a month. What patterns do you see? Do you like to reflect and plan later in the day, or in the morning? How can you pace your learning and work to be more productive?

3. Reflect on your strengths as a teacher. What learning theories or frameworks do you use when creating impactful learning experiences?

4. Create a concept map to examine your own beliefs about how learning happens. What does the term "learning sciences" mean to you?

5. Spend a day as your student, viewing learning through your students' eyes.

FIELDWORK

Observe Other Educators

See learning in a formal context in a new way. Visit a colleague and observe their teaching. Consider yourself an *ethnographer*—someone who studies cultures. Before you start this activity, think about how you'd like to record what you see—the data. There are classroom culture inventories available that will help you organize your thoughts. Traditionally, however, ethnographers take copious notes to form a rich, detailed description of the happenings (Ponterotto, 2006), which they then analyze within the sociocultural context.

1. Describe elements of the classroom culture. Are learning routines clearly visible? How would you characterize the learning context?

2. In your "snapshot" or visit, is the learning context equitable? How are all students involved in the learning community? Are any students not involved?

3. Consider the layout of the classroom. How are the desks/learning groups organized? What kind of visuals are in the room? Do they enhance or distract from learning?

4. Compare your teaching context with your colleague's context. Which of your practices do you think would be helpful to your colleague? Which of your colleague's practices would you like to try in your classroom or learning community?

Practice allowing your students to bring in their out-of-school learning interests and passions using an open, constructivist-inspired assignment. For example, have students write, blog, journal, or present on the skills they're learning while engaging in a favorite weekend activity.

Learn More:
Resources for Further Exploration

The learning classroom: *Theory into practice* (bit.ly/2ZnBQTd)

Digital Academic: *Digitally blooming—taxonomies for a digital age* (bit.ly/2RgG1NS)

Smithsonian Educatiom: How People Learn [Video] (youtu.be/SYFAh656WCs)

Kathy Schrock's Bloomin Apps [including resources aligned to Bloom's Taxonomy] (schrockguide.net/bloomin-apps.html)

Simply Psychology: *Skinner—Operant conditioning* (simplypsychology.org/operant-conditioning.html)

Sense and Sensation: *The cognitive science of education* (bit.ly/2WBpIfy)

Deep Dive

Hess, K. (2008). *Developing and using learning progressions as a schema for measuring progress.* Retrieved from nciea.org/publications/CCSSO2_KH08.pdf

Annenberg Learner: *Neuroscience & the Classroom* (learner.org/courses/neuroscience/text/text.html)

Schunk, D. H. (2012). *Learning Theories: an Educational Perspective*, sixth edition. Pearson.

Weinstein, Y., Sumeracki, M., & Caviglioli, O. (2018). *Understanding How We Learn: A Visual Guide*. Routledge.

CHAPTER 3

Digital Age Learners: Mind, Brain, and Cognition

Designing educational experiences without knowledge of the brain is like designing a glove without knowledge of the hand.

—LESLIE HART

In this chapter, we discuss the types of learner characteristics and capacities that impact learning. We discuss learner cognition and how our brains work, learner thinking, as well as socioemotional factors. We explore components that either facilitate learning, such, as positive mindsets, or detract from learners' capacities, such as some of the effects of poverty and other adverse childhood events. We also examine the idea of learning as being an inherently social activity—and what this means for individuals or groups of learners. These factors, learner characteristics and sociocultural context, comprise two branches of the Learner element of the LITE framework (Figure 3.1). Studies in human development, neuroscience, and cognitive sciences inform our knowledge about the processes of human learning. Educators must also consider the impact of culture and context.

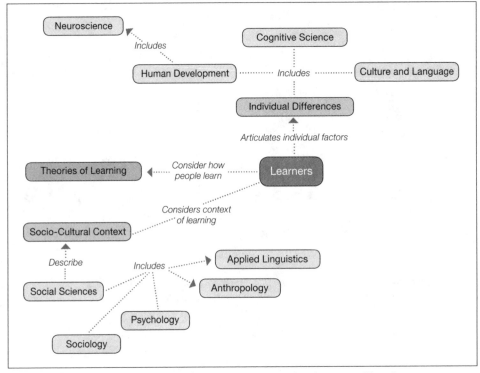

Figure 3.1 | Individual differences in learners and the sociocultural context of learning.

By the end of this chapter, you will be able to:

- Articulate the importance for educators to understand the basics of how the brain works for effective instruction.

- Explain, in general terms, the cognitive processes of learning (encoding, storage, and retrieval) including the roles of memory and attention.

- Reflect upon aspects of human development that may impact learners in their contexts.

- Describe the instructional ramifications of neuroplasticity.

- Explain the impact of motivation and social-emotional factors upon learning.

- Evaluate your understanding of how the brain works and dispel neuro-myths from your own practice.

ISTE Standards Connection

The following ISTE Standards are addressed in this chapter:

ISTE Standards for Educators

Citizen 3.a. Create experiences for learners to make positive, socially responsible contributions and exhibit empathetic behavior online that build relationships and community.

Collaborator 4.d. Demonstrate cultural competency when communicating with students, parents, and colleagues and interact with them as co-collaborators in student learning.

Designer 5.a. Use technology to create, adapt and personalize learning experiences that foster independent learning and accommodate learner differences and needs.

Designer 5.b. Design authentic learning activities that align with content area standards and use digital tools and resources to maximize active deep learning.

Understanding Your Learners

Learning scientists consider the impact of cognitive development, sociocultural context, the use of language and linguistics, psychological and emotional development, and other factors for individual and collective learner experiences. So what are busy teachers to do in designing effective learning experiences when learners vary in so many ways? Consider the theories of learning we've explored as we go on to examine some of the learner variables or differences. You may recognize some of the ideas from your work as a preservice teacher, but bear in mind your different frame of reference as an inservice teacher—your experience will now add to your understanding and you will comprehend the concepts differently. How do learners differ and why does it matter?

As educators, we intuitively understand that each learner is different, but we rarely talk about specific differences—except for perhaps preferences or (in error) learning styles. The fact is, the ways in which learners vary and how this impacts their learning processes is extremely complex. At the most fundamental level, we might consider behaviors, cognitive processes (thinking), affective responses (social-emotional), and stages of both physical and cognitive development (human development) differ for each learner. Then, if we consider learning to be primarily an individual sense-making process, where learners construct their meaning by building upon prior knowledge and experience, we must also consider:

- Brain development and neuroplasticity
- How learning works from a perspective of learner cognition
- The impact of socioemotional factors and motivation
- The impact of sociocultural factors and family life
- Mindsets and dispositions
- The role of prior knowledge and learning experiences

Human Development

The field of human development is concerned with understanding the typical patterns or trajectories (pathways) of change in physical, cognitive, emotional, and social growth. Learners' readiness to engage in tasks can be affected by developmental factors such as the development of gross and fine motor skills, proprioception (how learners perceive themselves in space), as well as cognitive (ways of thinking) and affective (emotional) development.

Most educators are familiar with some concepts of human development, both physical and cognitive, from studying the works of Jean Piaget or Erik Erikson as preservice teachers. Piaget and Erikson help us understand how the brain thinks and processes the world. These theories have been informed by careful observation and years of in-depth research. The main difference between their theories is that Piaget developed a theory that relates to the stages of childhood development—infancy to the teenage years, while Erikson was concerned with events progressing throughout life (Kail & Cavanuagh, 2008). Both theorists focused on stages of development and the sequential nature of these stages. Piaget's focus was on cognitive development, while Erikson's writings were more focused on emotional development, particularly that of infants through adulthood.

As a cognitive psychologist, Piaget believed that children and infants play an active role in the learning process. Much of Piaget's work in the area of cognitive development of children was influenced by his observations of his own daughter and nephew. Piaget's work was one of the first in the field to distinguish that the way children think is different from the way adults think. Piaget's theory of cognitive development proposes four stages of development:

1. **Sensorimotor stage:** birth to 2 years

2. **Preoperational stage:** ages 2 to 7

3. **Concrete operational stage:** ages 7 to 11

4. **Formal operational stage:** ages 12 and up (Piaget, J. 1971a)

Each stage has major characteristics that define the state of cognitive development. At the sensorimotor stage, an infant knows the world through movement and sensations. At the preoperational stage, children still think in concrete terms, but there is growth in language development and thinking. During the concrete operational stage, children begin to think logically about concrete events. Their thinking becomes more logical and organized. At the formal operational stage, children's thinking involves an increase in logic and they develop the ability to use deductive reasoning and understand abstract ideas (Piaget, J. 1971a).

Erikson, a developmental psychologist and psychoanalyst, is known for his theory on the psychosocial development of human beings. He was interested in how social interaction and relationships played a role in the development and growth of humans. He placed a strong emphasis on sociocultural factors because he believed they strongly influence development. Erikson's theory described the impact of social experience across one's entire lifespan.

Erikson also collaborated with his wife, Joan Erikson, to develop a comprehensive psychoanalytic theory that identifies a series of eight stages of development, each with its own psychological struggle, that a healthy individual passes through, from infancy to late adulthood:

Infancy: trust versus mistrust

Early childhood: autonomy versus shame and doubt

Preschool: initiative versus guilt

School age: industry versus inferiority

Adolescence: identity versus role confusion

Young adulthood: intimacy versus isolation

Middle adulthood: generativity versus stagnation

Maturity: ego integrity versus despair

By studying the works and theories of Piaget and Erikson, we are informed of pedagogical methods. Examining ideas from both theorists can help us construct a holistic view of the stages of development learners pass through. Taking into account both the cognitive and affective domains of human development guides us in understanding learning as a social act and assists us in understanding the implications for the classroom.

Digital Age Learners and the Brain

Understanding certain aspects of how our brains work and the conditions under which they function well for learning can lead to powerful insights for teachers. A policy report from the Royal Society (2011) stated that the common ground between education and neuroscience suggests a future in which educational practice can be transformed by science, just as medical practice was transformed by science about a century ago.

When educators think of brain development, we are primarily considering the level of development in mental or cognitive processes. According to evidence from educational neuroscience research, there are sensitive periods of development or growth in which "the brain is particularly susceptible to certain environmental stimuli and particularly efficient at processing and assimilating new information." (Blakemore, Grossmann, Cohen-Kadosh, Sebastian, & Johnson, 2013, p. 289) The brain is particularly sensitive to external stimuli in early childhood and the teenage years, which coincide with periods of *neural blooming*, when the development of neurons and the brain's information and relay systems are particularly active.

When learning occurs, connections between the neurons in the brain are strengthened. Judy Willis, a neurologist and middle school teacher, explains the continual growth of these connections through the formation of *dendrites*:

> Although most of the neurons where information is stored are present at birth, there is lifelong growth of the support and connecting cells that enrich the communication between neurons. These dendrites sprout from the arms (axons) or the cell body of the neuron. Dendrites increase in size and number in response to learned skills, experience, and information. (2006, p. 1)

However, over time, and at specific times of development, the connections that aren't used with any regularity are *pruned*. Willis continues:

Just as hedges are pruned to cut off errant shoots, the brain prunes its own inactive cells. How our brains accomplish this is fascinating—if cells are inactive, the blood flow around them diminishes, permitting a build-up of calcium ions, which in turn releases an enzyme causing the cells to self-destruct (2006, p. 2).

As you might have recognized, this is the biochemical process behind the adage "Use it or lose it," and understanding a brain-based process like this, even at the most basic level, can guide your instruction. Knowing this information, you can prioritize the building of connections and understand why we seem to lose access to the information if it isn't retrieved, thereby allowing the neural connections to atrophy or be pruned.

In a literal sense, our experiences shape the physical characteristics of our brains and therefore our perceptions, understanding, and cognitive capacities. Pioneering author Leslie A. Hart was an early advocate of brain-compatible learning, publishing his seminal book *Human Brain and Human Learning* in 1983. As early as 2002, there was concern that large amounts of media (4–6 hours per day) rewired the brain, and perhaps not in the most beneficial manner (Hart, 2002).

Normal brain development depends, in part, upon children's experiences and environments, as well as healthy nutrition. For teachers, however, Hart had a special message, which is both practical and inspiring:

> If a student cannot do what you expect of them, take time to build the neural wiring and structures that will enable them to do what your curriculum expects. An analogy is keeping the high jump bar over their heads when they don't have the physical skills for jumping it at waist height. (p. 77)

For educators who may have believed that brain capacity could not be developed, this is a positive message of hope.

Unlearning and Relearning: Implications for Digital Age Learners

Two generations of learners have now grown up immersed in an information-rich, digitally-mediated world connected by information and communications technologies (ICT). This environment has had an impact—either directly or indirectly—on almost every learner for the past 25–30 years. If learners aren't directly working with new digital technologies in schools, they are undoubtedly impacted by the world around them, which is dominated by high-speed media, information, communications, and social media networks.

The content of what children learn, how they learn it, as well as the pace and format of that learning have changed from previous generations—and now, science has proved, so have our learners' brains. Consider our discussion on brain development being directly related to our experiences and environment. How might your learners be impacted by their digital environment? Something we often ask our teacher-learners to think about, to put it in perspective, is how their own learners, having created neural efficiencies around digital media and tools for learning, might experience their classes.

What kind of experiences do your digital age learners encounter in the classroom environment? Are they enduring the tedious and challenging work of literally unlearning their natural ways of learning—and having to relearn older or obsolete ways of knowledge creation? Or are they able to build upon a digitally-influenced framework of knowledge, skills, and capacities from out-of-school learning? What kind of environment do you want to create?

Learning and Cognition

Cognition refers to the mental processes involved in sense-making—literally making sense of our existing knowledge—our ideas and perceptions, as well as data acquired through the sensory systems and experience. The processes of cognition are primarily brain-based, impacting performance and learning. We use cognition, for example, when we actively listen, as well as when we daydream, read, calculate, reason, learn, understand languages, and perceive the color red. Cognitive processes deeply influence what we perceive, remember, and understand. They shape our mindset, thinking patterns, intellectual growth, learning habits, and worldview.

There are several important principles of cognitive science and cognitive psychology that are critical for educators to understand and consider when teaching. These principles often appear to be folded into best practices, for example, the idea that learners build new knowledge upon existing cognitive structures (prior knowledge) and that knowledge is tied to the context(s) in which the knowledge was learned (teachers must help with transfer to new contexts). Understanding how to apply cognitive principles in effective learning systems is powerful—allowing a tremendous amount of impact for educators through small, but thoughtful changes.

Educators who understand and leverage findings from the learning sciences will enhance their current practice. Understanding principles of cognition and learning is a great place to start.

> [T]he revolution in the study of the mind, usually called the cognitive revolution, is allowing us to enter a new era of human learning and teaching. This era does not reject the practical knowledge that has built up over millennia but greatly improves and enriches it. Good teachers and good learners may be born, but they cannot reach their potential, or anything close to it, without a deep understanding of the learning processes and how to enhance them. (Simon, 2000, p. 116)

Educators may conceptualize the brain as a thinking system that reaches conclusions through mostly logical processes. The truth is, however, that thinking is a slow and effortful process—our brains are designed to rely primarily on memory, where we store information and strategies. As cognitive scientist Daniel Willingham asserts in *Why Don't Students Like School* (2009), "Humans don't think very often because our brains are designed not for thought but for the avoidance of thought. Thinking is not only effortful ... it's also slow and unreliable" (p. 4). Technology thought-leader Cathy Davidson describes the Hebbian principle behind the axiom "neurons that fire together, wire together" in her book *Now You See It* (2011). She explained that:

> [L]earning occurs when neurons streamline into pathways and then streamline into other pathways, into efficient clusters that act in concert with one another ... This means the more we repeat certain patterns of behavior (that the firing together), the more those behaviors become rapid, then reflexive, then automatic (that's the wiring) ... The behaviors combine into patterns, so we don't have to think. (p. 46)

In short, the goal of our brains is to automate processes, thoughts, strategies, and pieces of knowledge through strengthening neural circuits. This results in more efficiencies, speeding up retrieval of knowledge, often without conscious thought—and freeing up the brain to pay attention to other tasks. That's why thinking is challenging, particularly when learning something new. That's also why learners' attention—the right kind of attention—is critical to effective learning. It is also why learners of all ages feel that learning something new can be a heavy lift in the beginning. It's particularly uncomfortable for adults because it can take some time to understand where the existing knowledge and new knowledge fit together.

It is important to guide students to deeper levels of thinking and analysis—the higher-order thinking skills of Bloom's Taxonomy of cognitive objectives. But in practice, it can be quite challenging to engage learners in thinking processes in the classroom. If you've tried to teach thinking and reasoning skills, which most educators do, you're not alone in considering it to be a difficult task. According to Willingham, some students don't like school because it's hard! The difficulty and demands to think are taxing because "your brain serves many purposes, and thinking is not what it does best ... compared to your ability to see and move, thinking is slow, effortful and uncertain" (2009, p. 4). This cognitive reality explains the necessity of engaging learner interest, curiosity, and motivation to complete tasks.

Impactful Ideas from Cognitive Science

Two areas in the field of cognitive science are especially relevant to education: attention and memory. Understanding the basics of how these cognitive functions work can help educators tremendously by giving them insight into designing impactful instruction.

Attention

The act of paying attention is quite complex, involving the brain's attention systems that determine if information should continue to be processed and how—either briefly in short term memory or stored in long-term memory. As educators, we may think of attention in terms of engagement, meaning sustained focus on a thing or activity. Engagement is necessary and valuable in learning because it puts the learner in a focused state. We can't learn without attention, and engagement leads to better learning because it means extended time on task or more attention to the work.

Our attention system is receiving data from our senses and internal systems all the time. The brain performs a form of triage, prioritizing and filtering data, and acts as an attention filter to allow the brain to focus on specific stimuli.

> Awareness is the attention of the moment. The subconscious mind needs to be on autopilot to process the enormous amount of information from the world coming in through the senses. When our brains are working optimally, we recognize some input as familiar but unimportant and ignore it. We then automatically consider the data needing to be acknowledged at the moment. After brief consideration, the data are either dropped

from working memory and disregarded, or selected for further processing. (Willis, 2006, p. 39)

It is essential for educators to understand how cognitive processes and attention systems are involved, because of the important implications for learning environments. For example:

We've all had that experience—talking to someone who assures us they are listening, but it feels like nobody is home. We think of this as selective attention, but the learner may have simply tuned out due to boredom or perceived familiarity with the discussion. It's important for educators to understand how the brain's attention system scans for difference in information—that is, changes. Strategies which help to focus learners' attention introduce new, interesting information, which essentially signals the brain to prioritize this data. Practice in the process of focusing attention strengthens our abilities to maintain focus and "makes these circuits stronger so they are more efficiently accessed when needed" (Willis, 2006, p. 39).

If learners filter out your learning activity, it could be because they are on autopilot and not stimulated to pay focused attention. In a famous experiment, psychologists Simons and Chabris (1999) tested an idea related to the concept known as selective attention. To take the test yourself, see the sidebar How Well Do You Pay Attention before reading any farther (spoiler alert!).

Selective attention can lead to attention blindness, where while concentrating so hard on some details, we miss others. In their famous "invisible gorilla" experiment, Simons and Chabris asked viewers to focus on a basketball that was passed between two color-coded teams, to determine how many times the ball was passed amongst the white team. During play, a person in a gorilla suit wanders through the middle of the court but remained unnoticed by half of all viewers. It is a powerful demonstration of selective attention and attention blindness. Unless you've experienced the phenomenon yourself, it is difficult to imagine how viewers could miss seeing the gorilla—which lingers on the screen for nine seconds.

Attention blindness has important implications for educational practice. According to Davidson (2011),

> If things are habitual, we don't pay attention to them—until they become a problem. Attention

HOW WELL DO YOU PAY ATTENTION?

Take the Selective Attention Test by Simons and Chabris to find out before continuing to read about attention. (youtu.be/vJG698U2Mv)

is about difference. We pay attention to things that are not part of our automatic repertoire of responses, reflexes, concepts, preconceptions, behaviors, knowledge. (p. 49)

For educators to entice, leverage, and sustain the attention of learners, the learning environment and activities must be designed to maintain interest and allow for the active construction of knowledge. The desire to pay attention is closely entwined with learner motivation (Bransford, 2000).

Memory

When we think about memory, we may think of distinct areas of the brain where complete and accurate memories reside. In fact, the entire brain is involved in creating memories. And when we remember, our memories are not merely retrieved, they are reconstructed, which leaves them vulnerable to inaccuracies and subjective influences.

While there are several kinds of memory; including episodic, semantic, explicit, implicit, and procedural; when we describe learning processes that involve memory, we primarily refer to short- or long-term memory and encoding.

Short term memory functions as a short term holding space for the brain to make decisions about where to send the information for additional processing—or not. In a brief amount of time (roughly 15–30 seconds), our minds decide whether to pay attention to some incoming data for further processing, or to filter it out. Long term memory can be thought of data that has been encoded and stored in a way that can be retrieved. Encoding permits the new knowledge to be available as a memory.

It is important for educators to have a general understanding of these processes to optimize their teaching. In particular, teachers should understand:

- The idea that learning happens within contexts and circumstances which are comingled and associated through memory formation
- The impact of being distracted on short term memory
- The idea of cognitive load (how taxed the brain is during learning activities)
- The role of prior information in memory
- The role of guided and distributed practice in building neural connections and enhancing retrieval

- The idea of transfer of learning, how explicit connections of concepts are needed between contexts to strengthen associations and hence retrieval

- The use of teaching strategies based upon findings from the cognitive sciences, such as interleaving content, elaboration, and concrete examples to help to strengthen memory by building and fostering connections between existing and new knowledge

- The effective use of digital tools and technologies to act as cognitive extensions, in that they free up available working memory by lessening learners' cognitive load—effectively increasing capacity for example, a spreadsheet enabling "if –then" analysis, or modeling objects in 3D space such as augmented or virtual reality

Where and how memories are stored is highly significant. Consider, for example, where you store important but infrequently used decorations, pans, or tools in your home. Having access is important—and how the items are organized makes a huge difference in how long it takes to retrieve them. Perhaps it is most important to recall the last time you used the items, possibly for a family event (which makes you smile!) in order to remember that you lent the pans to your mother who left them in the garage, not the usual place. This is analogous to the ways our memories work in that, "Memory storage is more efficient when the new information is related to prior knowledge. The more memories in the storage bank, the more neuron circuits there are to connect with the new information" (Willis, 2006, p. 39). Sometimes, connections must be made explicitly to existing knowledge so that new knowledge can be assimilated into existing memory structures.

As educators know intuitively, emotions play a key role in learning. It's only recently, however, that the connections between cognition, learning, and emotion have been recognized. For example, we understand now that while a small amount of stress is helpful during learning, significant stress impairs the encoding processes of building memories. Conversely, positive emotions can enhance performance of cognitive functions (Hardiman, 2012).

Prior Knowledge

Educators often consider the idea of background or prior knowledge when teaching, but not usually from the perspective that our learners have existing knowledge categories and associations upon which we must build. As Bransford, Cocking, and colleagues explained:

A logical extension of the view that new knowledge must be constructed from existing knowledge is that teachers need to pay attention to the incomplete understandings, the false beliefs, and the naive renditions of concepts that learners bring with them to a given subject. Teachers then need to build on these ideas in ways that help each student achieve a more mature understanding. If students' initial ideas and beliefs are ignored, the understandings that they develop can be very different from what the teacher intends. (2000, p. 22)

It is crucial for educators working at all levels—including professional development and higher education—to elicit learners' prior knowledge—their models of understanding—and then to determine the accuracy of this knowledge. Without uncovering possible misconceptions, new knowledge will not be built upon an accurate or logical foundation. To discover learners' prior understandings, educators can use strategies such as pre-tests, short discussions on key or frequently misunderstood topics, and visual representations or models to describe concepts.

Neuroplasticity

It's difficult to imagine that until the end of the 20th century, the prevailing belief was that attributes of the brain—such as the ability to learn particular skills—were fixed. In other words, there was a general consensus that the brain remained much the same throughout life, with limited growth and development. Beliefs about intelligence were similar; we were born with a distinct level of intelligence, inherited from our parents, and this was a quality that was fixed throughout our lives, barring injury or illness. The important work of psychologist Carol Dweck and her colleagues examined the role of such beliefs, referred to as mindsets, in learning and achievement. Their work found significant differences in skill development and growth between learners who had a *fixed* mindset, meaning they believed their potential for achievement was predetermined or fixed, and learners who had a *growth* mindset, meaning they believed in their ability to improve (Dweck, 2008).

The idea of a growth mindset, that our applied intelligence or cognitive capacities can improve or grow, is transformational for learners. It is based upon the idea of *neuroplasticity,* or the idea that learning changes the physical structures of the brain throughout life—not only during youth and adolescence. David Sousa, international consultant on educational neuroscience, writes about this important finding, stating "... the human brain continually reorganizes itself on the basis of input. The process, called neuroplasticity, continues throughout our life but is exceptionally rapid in the early years" (2017, p. 5). For both learners and educators, the implications of believing improvement—real growth—in skills and knowledge is possible, can be life-changing.

What Are Neuromyths?

When educators' practices are informed by research-backed knowledge about mind, brain, and education—a growing subset of the learning sciences—the impact can be powerful. However, when findings of studies are taken out of context or misapplied, the resulting *neuromyths*, or misconceptions about how the brain or its processes work, can have undesirable effects when applied in learning contexts. Initially defined by the Organisation for Economic Co-operation and Development (OECD) in its *Understanding the Brain: Towards a New Learning Science* report (2007), the neuromyths and their implications were further explained:

> These misconceptions often have their origins in some element of sound science, which makes identifying and refuting them the more difficult. As they are incomplete, extrapolated beyond the evidence, or plain false, they need to be dispelled in order to prevent education running into a series of dead-ends. (p. 16)

So where do neuromyths come from? For a number of reasons, misconceptions about the brain and learning are quite prevalent, both among the general public and educators. Problems arise when research findings are taken out of context or misapplied, often quite unintentionally. For example, the popular belief in learning styles—specifically that individuals have preferred modes of learning through which they learn more effectively—is a neuromyth:

> Despite the popularity of learning styles and inventories such as the VARK, it's important to know that there is no evidence to support the idea that matching activities to one's learning style improves learning ... for years researchers have tried to make this connection through hundreds of studies. (Chick, n.d.)

In fact, despite the idea of learning styles being refuted repeatedly (Gutiérrez & Rogoff, 2003; Willingham, 2005, 2018; Pashler, McDaniel, Rohrer, & Bjork, 2008; Dembo, & Howard, 2007, Kirschner, 2017), it remains a popular belief among educators.

Another common reason for the persistence of neuromyths is the assumption that when two things happen together (correlate), one factor causes the other (causation). Correlation however, does not always mean there is a causal relationship, where one is the reason for the other. Both the crime rate and rate of ice cream sales increase in the summer (and when the weather is warmer in general). This is an association or correlation, meaning the two phenomena occur together somehow, not causation. We wouldn't say that eating ice cream causes crime!

Dispelling neuromyths is challenging because they are pervasive and may have origins in scientific research. Some teachers learn about these beliefs in their preservice education, shared by well-intended teacher educators who hold common misconceptions or outdated information about the brain. Other neuromyths are perpetuated by popular educational programs that claim to be "brain-based" but are not grounded by evidence or scientific validation. Educators are urged to exercise caution in evaluating claims of brain-based products. Harvard University Graduate School of Education researchers Sylvan and Christodoulou suggested that clarification is needed to distinguish brain-based attribution such as brain-based educational theories, principles and corresponding instructional techniques and educational products, due to confusion around terminology (2010, p. 2). In a 2012 study, Dekker and colleagues Lee, Howard-Jones, and Jolles conducted research to identify possible predictive factors for teachers' understanding of neuromyths:

> Results showed that on average, teachers believed 49% of the neuromyths, particularly myths related to commercialized educational programs.... These findings suggest that teachers who are enthusiastic about the possible application of neuroscience findings in the classroom find it difficult to distinguish pseudoscience from scientific facts.

Dekker et al.'s research affirms the growing interest in educators about the findings of learning sciences, educational neuroscience, and mind, brain, and education studies. However, a troubling finding of the study was that general knowledge of the brain was a predictor for who scored higher in believing common misconceptions or neuromyths (Dekker, Lee, Howard-Jones, & Jolles, 2012).

In the teaching context, belief in these neuromyths can lead to practices which are ineffective as well as purchase of curriculum materials and instructional technologies that are based on pseudoscience instead of evidence-based principles. In addition to wasting time and money, a serious consequence may be the formation of misconceptions informing teachers' practice and ultimately, the learners' understanding.

Table 3.1 shares several examples of popular misconceptions about how the brain works and responses from research to disprove them.

Table 3.1 | (Neuro)myth Busting Popular Ideas about the Brain

MISCONCEPTION OR NEUROMYTH	(NEURO)MYTH BUSTING
1. People who are able to multitask are more efficient. Learners in the digital age are skilled at multitasking.	When we think we are multitasking, we are actually switching between two tasks. This incurs a mental cost in speed and accuracy as the brain adjusts between tasks. Younger learners appear to more successfully multitask than older—that is, experience less loss of speed and accuracy—because of a larger capacity of working memory. "Multitasking isn't a good idea if you really want to get something done," (Willingham, 2010, p. 26).
2. People are born with a finite number of brain cells. As adults we do not generate additional brain cells.	Although believed true until quite recently, we now know that adults are capable of neurogenesis or growth of new brain cells.
3. Learners learn more effectively when taught in their preferred learning style.	This myth has been discredited for over a decade, but the belief persists among educators and others. Now, we recognize that although learners may have preferences for a learning mode, it may not be the best through which to understand the content at hand.
4. At any one time, we use 10% of our brains.	This myth originated from a misinterpretations of brain images. Hot spots of activity, which appear as dense spots of color, were mistaken as the only site of brain activity at the time, which is false.
5. Our intelligence is determined at birth by genetics and is fixed.	For a long time, it was believed that intelligence was inherited and that our capacities are fixed. Researcher Carol Dweck has disputed this belief and shares evidence from her work which demonstrates that the belief that one's mindset is not fixed—ie. that our mental capacity can grow—that is critical for 21st century learners.
6. Right or left brain domination explains differences in learners, e.g. logical or creative.	While specialized regions of the brain may be located mostly on one side of the brain, the two hemispheres actually work together. There is no truth to the belief in hemispheric dominance such as right-brained people are more creative or left-brained are more logical.

Continued

MISCONCEPTION OR NEUROMYTH	(NEURO)MYTH BUSTING
7. After critical periods of development, some skills can no longer be learned.	This is false. We can always learn new skills, but at different rates than during certain periods of development.
8. Listening to classical music while working increases children's reasoning abilities or general intelligence.	The so-called Mozart effect, the claims that listening to classical music increases general intelligence or reasoning skills, originated when a study by Rauscher, Shaw, & Ky (1993) was misinterpreted and decontextualized. One of the study findings was a temporary (10-15 minute) cognitive gain in temporal spatial test performance in adults when listening to one particular composition by Mozart. (Rauscher & Hinton, 2006)
9. Memories are stored in specialized regions of the brain only.	After memories are encoded, long-term memories are stored in networks across the brain.
10. A sensitive period for brain development, such as adolescence, means certain skills must be learned at this time or can never be learned.	While there are sensitive periods of rapid development and brain reorganization, it is not true that certain skills—such as language, or playing a musical instrument—must be learned at certain times. We can continue to learn new skills during periods of normal brain development, at different rates.

So, why then do myths persist? Consider the incorrect belief about students' learning styles—which has been repeatedly studied, but has no robust evidence to be true. In continuing to create practices around the idea, teachers are looking for solutions, suggest Willingham, Hughes, and Dobolyi (2015). If teachers fixated on the idea that every student is completely unique, they contend, that would lead to paralysis. For teachers, a compromise is seemingly the idea of learning styles—principles which apply to groups of students, but can be assessed individually, a kind of middle ground.

Professor Tokuhama-Espinosa, who teaches the science of mind, brain, and education studies at Harvard Extension, considered a teacher-friendly and practical approach in her newly published work, *Neuromyths: Debunking False Ideas about the Brain* (2018). In the book, she explains the probable origins of many misconceptions and clarifies concepts in a teacher-friendly way. She also explains the relationship of the learning sciences to these disciplines in an engaging video (see the Learn More section at the end of this chapter).

Such approaches use different scholarly lenses to consider how brain processes impact learning and knowledge acquisition. While the approaches are different, there are commonalities such as the emphasis on educating holistically, the importance of emotions in learning and accounting for the environment—for which educators have long advocated. In addition to Tokuhama-Espinosa, cognitive psychologist Daniel Willingham and neurologist-turned-middle-school-teacher Judy Willis present findings from neurology useful for educators in a practical, teacher-friendly manner. As the relatively new branches of the study of learning sciences (such as mind, brain, and education (MBE) and educational neuroscience) influence the field of educator preparation, this may result in more attention to the evidence in evidence-based practices. See the Learn More section for additional resources.

LEARNING AND THE BRAIN: A FUN QUIZ

How much do you know about learning and the brain? Take this fun quiz to test your knowledge of neuromyths! (goo.gl/BxMM9N)

Motivation

How does learner motivation impact learning? What is motivation and how can educators motivate their students? All learners need some sort of motivation to learn but teachers have always struggled to motivate learners. Researchers on motivation are working to help them by examining what learners want and what motivates them. The answers are incredibly complex. According to educational researcher Lai (2011):

> Motivation refers to reasons that underlie behavior that is characterized by willingness and volition. Intrinsic motivation is animated by personal enjoyment, interest, or pleasure, whereas extrinsic motivation is governed by reinforcement contingencies. Motivation involves a constellation of closely related beliefs, perceptions, values, interests, and actions. (Abstract)

There are two types of motivation, intrinsic and extrinsic. Extrinsic motivation pertains to actions undertaken to achieve external consequences such as grades or rewards and has a performance goal orientation. Intrinsic motivation refers to doing an activity simply for the enjoyment of the activity itself, rather than its instrumental value (Ryan and Deci, 2000) and has a learning goal orientation. Both kinds of motivation are useful in the classroom but learners vary widely as to what they find motivating—and when! Motivation can be contextual or situational and so inherently, it is variable, even for individuals. This is part of the difficulty.

As educators, we should also consider the potential of our instruction to *demotivate* learners. Increasingly our youth—particularly teens—are disengaged and demotivated within formal educational contexts because they view them as irrelevant and disconnected from their cultural contexts (Ito et al., 2013). Many young people feel disconnected from structured learning settings—a situation that apparently has persisted for decades. Writing in 1966, Bruner described a similar concern which impacted the motivation to learn. In *Toward a Theory of Instruction* he described:

> The will to learn is an intrinsic motive, one that finds both its source and its reward in its own exercise. The will to learn becomes a 'problem' only under specialized circumstances like those of a school, where a curriculum is set, students confined, and a path fixed. The problem exists, not so much in the learning itself, but in the fact that what the school imposes often fails to enlist the natural energies that sustain spontaneous learning—curiosity, a desire for competence, aspiration to emulate a model. (p. 127)

If learners are disengaged from the content and context of learning, particularly in the context of classroom learning, they may experience *stressful boredom* and may respond by developing negative associations with the topics (Willis, 2014). As Dörnyei (2001) commented, "... Motivation is highest when students are competent, have sufficient autonomy, set worthwhile goals, get feedback and are affirmed by others ... For many, demotivation has more impact than motivation" (as cited in Hattie., 2009, p. 48).

Learning and Emotions

Carol Dweck (2007) has been on the forefront of research into how social emotional learning and the growth mindset can impact learning. After decades of research, Dweck discovered a simple but groundbreaking idea: the power of mindset. People who have developed a *fixed mindset*—those who believe that abilities are fixed—are less likely to flourish academically, socially, and economically than those with a *growth mindset*—those who believe that abilities can be developed. Dweck's book *Mindset* reveals how great parents, teachers, managers, and athletes can put this idea to use to foster outstanding accomplishment.

According to Dweck, a growth mindset creates a love for learning and a resilience that is essential for great accomplishments. Having a growth mindset means that we take on challenges wholeheartedly, learn from our setbacks and try again. We won't be able to avoid difficult situations, but we can be prepared with strategies when they strike.

For example, being mindful of our language—praising effort towards a goal, providing corrective feedback so learners can see themselves approaching the goal, or sharing information about how our brains continue to grow and how that impacts learner knowledge. Also, as educators, it's crucial to be mindful of instructional strategies that will set up learners for success—such as understanding learner readiness for new content, or the extent of prior knowledge.

Adverse Childhood Experiences and the Lifelong Consequences of Trauma

In order to develop healthy problem solving and coping skills, children need to experience *some* emotional stress in the early years; however, too much stress can be far more harmful than you might think. Experts categorize stress as *positive*, helping to guide growth; *tolerable*, which, while not helpful, will cause no permanent damage; or *toxic*, which is sufficient to overcome the child's undeveloped coping mechanisms and lead to long-term impairment and illness. Important research has been conducted in many fields (neuroscience, behavioral science, sociology, and medicine) on the effect of traumatic stress on brain development. Healthy brain development can be disrupted or impaired by prolonged, pathologic stress response with significant and lifelong implications for learning, behavior, health, and adult functioning (Shonkoff, 2012).

Adverse childhood experiences (ACEs) are stressful or traumatic events, including abuse and neglect. They may also include household dysfunction such as witnessing domestic violence or growing up with family members who have substance use disorders. ACEs are strongly related to the development and prevalence of a wide range of health problems throughout a person's lifespan, including those associated with substance misuse (SAMHSA, 2019). ACEs can disrupt the development of brain and other organ systems, increasing the risk of stress-related disease and cognitive impairment well into the adult years.

Adverse childhood experiences include

- Abuse: emotional, physical, and sexual

- Neglect: emotional and physical
- Mother treated violently
- Household substance abuse
- Household mental illness
- Parental separation or divorce
- Incarcerated household member

Understanding the research on ACEs can inform teachers of the importance of assessing the emotional climate of the classroom as we design powerful learning environments for all learners. Research shows that when students develop their capacity for emotional awareness, along with strategies for emotional regulation, their behavior and academic performance improve (Mendelson et al., 2015).

Research has also shown that students who have endured ACEs are significantly more likely to exhibit behavioral issues such as externalizing (aggression, poor impulse control, etc.) or internalizing (withdrawal, shutting down, etc.) Burke et al,

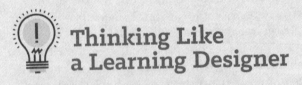

Thinking Like a Learning Designer

Are Gold Stars Really Effective?

Mia is a 2nd-grade teacher with several years' experience. She uses weekly behavior charts that she displays in the classroom. She has noticed that if students do well at the beginning of the week, when there is a new chart, they continue to collect the gold stars for good behavior for the rest of the week. A certain group of students, however, become discouraged if they do not earn gold stars on the first day or two and are even more disruptive throughout the rest of the week.

Questions for Reflection

- What is teacher Mia actually rewarding with the stars?
- Would you use this system, and if so, under which circumstances?

2011). These behaviors are a form of communication that tells us that our students need to feel a safe environment in their classrooms. Building and maintaining healthy relationships is often difficult for children who experience ACEs. However, educators have the opportunity to create and design classroom environments that nurture resiliency for our most vulnerable students.

Chapter Takeaways

- Attention must be specifically directed towards learning targets.

- Educators must be mindful of memory limitations and structures when teaching.

- Persistent neuromyths can be sources of misconceptions for teachers.

- Emotion, motivation, and learner beliefs impact learning.

- Educators can use familiar and new strategies to optimize learning with the way the brain works in mind.

- Toxic levels of stress and trauma interfere with cognitive systems, impacting memory formation.

Suggested Activities

1. What does paying attention look like in your home or classroom? Offline: Step back and observe explicitly looking for signs of attentiveness or inattentiveness. Online: record a session, or have a colleague record a session and review.

2. Teacher as ethnographer: Attention blindness and culture. What is ethnography and how can it help teachers learn about their classroom cultures? Can you train your students to also be observers and ethnographers? Try asking them to describe homework, bedtime, or dinner habits. It's a good idea to share your record of the same kind of event for student learners.

3. Learner 360: For this activity, observe one or more of your learners in three different learning contexts using observations. Then, create learner profiles, analyzing the information (data) you collected.

4. Just Asking: Learner Agency and Voice. Ask students what motivates them in a survey or poll—share data and ask learners what they think it means in terms of action steps.

FIELDWORK

Learner Landscape Activity

The main idea here is to understand how the learner applies strategies in different learning contexts, and how characteristics such as motivation and persistence change. You may wish to work in a team setting for this activity, to share findings with colleagues.

1. Select one or two students to study, comparing and contrasting their learning behaviors in different contexts to get a "360" view. How do they learn in different environments? Select students who are active in extracurricular activities or self-directed learning.

2. *Keep it simple!* Access is key here—parents may welcome an opportunity to talk about their child's learning habits (it happens at most parent-teacher conferences!). Plan B is to seek an adult to work with.

3. Investigate patterns of learning in 3 or 4 differently learning contexts. Include questions about level and kind of motivation, what happens when learning is hard? (persistence-at-task, do they give up or push through?), student comfort level etc.

4. Interview activity leaders (10–15 minutes). Interview parents about child's self-directed learning at home using digital tools. Interview child about child's learning habits.

5. Observe students in other classes, or adults while playing their favorite games.

6. Compile your observations as a short report of 3–5 pages. Compare and contrast learner strategies, approach and characteristics in each environment—individually, or as a synthesis.

7. Use pictures, graphs, or other images, if helpful, to explain.

Learn More: Resources for Further Exploration

Learning Sciences

The Nature of Learning: Using Research to Inspire Practice, by H. Dumont, D. Istance, & F. Benavides

Attention Blindness

Daniel Simons: Seeing the world as it isn't [Video] (youtu.be/9Il_D3Xt9W0)

American Psychological Association: *Sights unseen* (apa.org/monitor/apr01/blindness.aspx)

Mind, Brain, and Education

Dr. Mariale Hardiman: The Brain-Targeted Teaching model [Video] (youtu.be/ZUbyi5Acc2U)

National Academies Press: *Misconceptions as barriers to understanding science* (nap.edu/read/5287/chapter/5)

Dr. Tracey Tokuhama-Espinosa: Neuromyths [Video] (youtu.be/ED_MdfkPONw

The difference between mind, brain and education, educational neuroscience and the learning sciences [Video] (youtu.be/nAGsJ3xP944)

Social-Emotional Topics

Common Sense Education: *Digital citizenship and social-emotional learning* (bit.ly/2QfqqOa)

Center of the Developing Child, Harvard University: *Toxic stress* (bit.ly/2XM0c8D)

Deep Dive

Annenberg Learner: Thinking about thinking: Metacognition [Course] (bit.ly/2WGphWh)

Ambrose, S. A., Bridges, M. W., DiPietro, M., Lovett, M. C., & Norman, M. K. (2010). *How learning works: Seven research-based principles for smart teaching.* John Wiley & Sons.

The Collaborative for Social and Emotional Learning (casel.org/csi-resources)

Dulak, J. Domitrovich, C. Weissberg, R. Gullotta T. (Eds.) (2016) *Handbook of Social and Emotional Learning- Research and Practice*. New York: Guilford Press.

Dweck, C. (2007). *Mindset: The new psychology of success*. New York: Ballantine Books.

Piaget, J. (1971a). The theory of stages in cognitive development. In D. Green, M. P. Ford, & G. B. Flamer (Eds.), *Measurement and Piaget* (pp. 1e11). New York: McGraw-Hill.

Piaget, J. (1976). *The grasp of consciousness*. Cambridge, MA: Harvard University

Piaget, J. (1981). *Intelligence and affectivity*. Palo Alto: Annual reviews, Inc. (Original work published 1954).

Piaget, J. (1987). *Possibility and necessity: The role of possibility in cognitive development*. Minneapolis: University of Minnesota Press (Original work published 1983).

Piaget, J. (2001). *The psychology of intelligence*. New York: Routledge.

CHAPTER 4

Effective Teaching for Digital Age Learning: Evidence-Based Practices

Eliminate or drastically reduce low-input materials and processes such as textbooks, worksheets, and working in isolation in the absence of large amounts of sensory input from experiences in the real world. Remember, dittos don't make dendrites!

—HART, 2002, P. 76

In this chapter, we explore the powerful evidence-based teaching practices that leverage student capacity for *deep* and *sticky* learning. We present how educators can support learners to take control of their learning, and share ideas about using digital technologies to enhance learning outcomes.

By the end of this chapter, you will be able to:

- Explain effective teaching which results in deep, sticky, transferable learning as well as fluency in 21st-century skills such as the 4C's

- Explain frameworks for research-based effective teaching strategies or high-level teaching practices (HLTP)

- Deconstruct and evaluate teaching practice and learner outcomes

- Explore ideas, constructs and strategies important for instruction

- Describe teaching as a design science and practice

- Explain the processes of collecting evidence of instructional impact through assessment and research methods

ISTE Standards Connection

The following ISTE Standards are addressed in this chapter:

ISTE Standards for Educators

Learner 1a. Set professional learning goals to explore and apply pedagogical approaches made possible by technology and reflect on their effectiveness.

Learner 1b. Pursue professional interests by creating and actively participating in local and global learning networks.

Leader 2c. Model for colleagues the identification, exploration, evaluation, curation and adoption of new digital resources and tools for learning.

Designer 5a. Use technology to create, adapt, and personalize learning experiences that foster independent learning and accommodate learner differences and needs.

Designer 5b. Design authentic learning activities that align with content area standards and use digital tools and resources to maximize active deep learning.

Designer 5c. Explore and apply instructional design principles to create innovative digital learning environments that engage and support learning.

Looking through the Learning Science Lens

At its most basic, learning involves change—a kind of neurological building. It is influenced by content and learners and is situated within context. For educators, working with groups of learners who each vary—and carefully facilitating and orchestrating all the micro-interactions in the class—their work is very complex. Understanding what works for teaching really boils down to what is effective for whom, in which learning context, all of which is dependent upon the learning goals, content, and pedagogical approaches. In essence, each learning context is its own ecosystem—with accompanying complexity.

Professor and educator Linda Darling-Hammond advocates for a kind of education that was more than "covering curriculum" and which sought "to bridge the needs and interests of each learner (1995)

> This [more complex] approach to teaching requires not only that teachers have a deep knowledge of subject matter and a wide repertoire of teaching strategies, but also that they have an intimate knowledge of students' growth, experiences, learning styles and development. This understanding of learners and learning, I would argue, is the most neglected aspect of teacher preparation in this country. (p. 9)

So what do we mean by *looking through the learning science lens*? We know there are many points of view through which to view learning, depending upon the field. For example, how would a sociologist or anthropologist or a cognitive scientist look at a particular learning situation? It's important for educators to consider the design science and practice of teaching as working together, and best viewed through a learning sciences, or science of learning perspective. Understanding the pertinent findings of the learning sciences, however, can be a challenge for educators because, according to Kim, McGivney, & Care),

> research on learning does not consistently inform the everyday practice of teachers, showing a further divide between learning sciences and schooling. To no fault of teachers, the science of learning is often not translated into digestible and practical strategies. (2017)

In this chapter, we briefly look at the goals and outcomes of education, frameworks of evidence-based instructional practices or constructs, and view instruction through the lens of educational psychology, cognitive sciences, and social psychology.

Goals of Effective Teaching

While the goals of curriculum and instruction vary depending on content and context, learner growth is always the desired learning outcome. We want our learners to grow in ways that can be measured and observed. Among the goals of effective teaching are to bring about understanding of targeted knowledge, skills, dispositions, and capacities such as curricular outcomes and educational standards. The practice of teaching, however, is infinitely complex with many variables. Here are some common goals of instruction that lead to learner growth:

- Share understanding of targeted knowledge, skills, dispositions, and capacities.

- Bridge prior knowledge to help learners in a sense-making process through which new information is sorted and linked to existing schema and memories.

- Help learners achieve deep learning, which has a lasting impact on memory.

- Promote learning that is transferable to other contexts (teachers may need to help learners connect contexts, for example, through analogy).

- Teach ways of thinking and skills that help students regulate their own learning.

- Move learners forward through learning progressions.

- Facilitate the process of making connections and transfering learning to other situations.

- Create effective strategies for content delivery.

To observe the results of learners' thinking, educators examine artifacts; it's not possible to actually see or measure thinking, but evidence of growth can be seen by looking at the products and processes of learning.

The most essential learning outcome, perhaps, is students who become independent, life-long learners; an informed citizenry who can be successful in life and work. The skills, knowledge, and dispositions needed to attain this outcome now are much different than even in the recent past. Tony Wagner of the Harvard School of Education shared his findings of seven survival skills articulated by business leaders as being essential for workers in global innovation economies:

1. Critical Thinking and Problem-Solving

2. Collaboration Across Networks and Leading by Influence

3. Agility and Adaptability

4. Initiative and Entrepreneurialism

5. Effective Oral and Written Communication

6. Accessing and Analyzing Information

7. Curiosity and Imagination (Wagner, n.d.)

Note that several of these skills are *ways of thinking.* Thinking about our work as educators, we don't often share strategies for thinking, critique ways of thinking, deliberately shape thinking, or talk about how we can create shifts in thinking. We speak mostly of teaching and learning, but the heart of our work is actually changing the brains of our learners by teaching them how to monitor their own thinking, think about familiar topics in new ways, or create new thinking. Neuroscientist Martha Burns explains in her February 19, 2019 EdSurge article, *I'm a Neuroscientist. Here's How Teachers Change Kids' Brains*:

> Teachers change brains. While we often don't think of ourselves as brain changers, when we teach we have an enormous impact on our students' cognitive development. Recent advances in educational neuroscience are helping educators understand the critical role we play in building brain capacities important to students' learning and self-control.

While teachers intuitively understand their role in building brain capacities—that is, brain changing—because of external pressures to perform, their focus must be the curriculum content and evidence of learning, often measured in standardized tests. Teaching learners how to think is challenging work—and work that cannot easily be measured—it has to be inferred through the students' products of learning. It's not difficult to understand that the kinds of thinking and knowledge acquisition tested are actually lower order thinking skills, primarily remembering declarative knowledge. For learners to demonstrate competencies in higher-order thinking skills (HOTS), content knowledge of the topic or subject is essential. Furthermore, these skills are more difficult to assess, particularly through standardized means. In the meantime, however, how are learners becoming independent thinkers and learners?

In a recent course in the learning sciences, Dr. Elkordy asked her graduate teacher-learners to share their thoughts about the importance of teaching habits of mind, such as learning how to learn and a positive (growth) mindset. The results, shown in Figure 4.1, demonstrate that 94.4% of respondents consider this to be essential (33.3%) or quite important (61.1%)—with only 5.6% indicating that the skills are helpful but not important for regular practice.

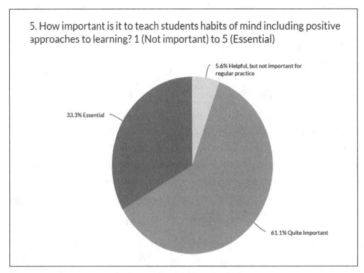

Figure 4.1 | Importance of teaching habits of mind.

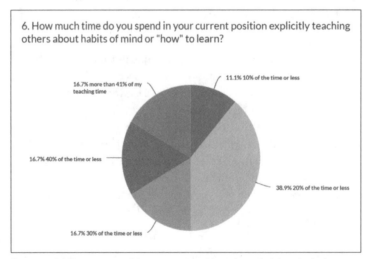

Figure 4.2 | Percentage of time spent teaching about habits of mind.

Despite the high value teachers assigned to the task, however, when they were asked to estimate the percentage of time they spent teaching these skills (Figure 4.2), the results were mixed.

These results aren't surprising. There are many reasons why teachers may not be devoting more time to teaching students how to learn: lack of time, conflicting priorities, incomplete knowledge of effective strategies and furthermore these skills are more difficult to assess, particularly through standardized means. In an article titled *Learning How to Learn* in the ISTE publication *Empowered Learner* (January, 2019), neuroscientist Melina Uncapher of the University of California, states that "part of the problem [in distilling research into classroom practices] is that 'the science of learning isn't systematically being taught to our teachers, which is terrifying.'"

For educators, the idea of integrating a new set of ideas from another discipline—the learning sciences—into their practice can be daunting. We suggest focusing first on developing learners' capacities to learn and then taking a mental step back from the best strategies to understand the key ideas from cognitive science that make these strategies work. We recommend that teachers focus on the following key concepts when developing their learners' capacities to learn independently:

Metacognition. Teach metacognitive practices through which leaners develop understanding of their own thinking (self-awareness, how they learn best, strategies for when they get stuck).

Goal setting. Teach goal setting skills and use the language of incremental movement towards accomplishing goals. (What is your learning goal? What's next?)

Self-regulation and self-monitoring/assessment. Self-regulation and associated executive function skills, such as staying on task, help learners to know when to persist, use strategies to stay on task, or ask for help.

Learning habits. Teach effective learning strategies based upon cognitive science—leveraging how the brain works.

Motivation. Be aware that motivation is a complex construct or idea, and is individual in nature. For example, depending upon whether learners have a performance orientation (just want to get it completed to earn the grade) or learning goal (true interest in comprehending the topic) will mean different motivations. Watch out for demotivating tasks, they have a powerfully negative effect on learning.

Independent learning. Encourage learners to take advantage of informal opportunities to pursue interest-based learning in the community and through web-based resources. Allow them to bring this learning into the classroom.

Growth mindset. Positive growth-mindsets are crucial for self-efficacy, a key predictor of success. Explain what to expect on the learning journey; explain what is happening and that learning isn't easy. Promote the idea of learning progressions, moving through stages from novice to expert as learners build knowledge over time.

Learner identity and self-concept. Guide students in developing strong learner identities and positive self-concepts. Help learners place themselves on learning trajectories in all subjects. Use language to describe learners as scholars, mathematicians, scientists, and explorers.

Reflective practices. Teach learners to examine their own learning through reflection strategies. Students should ask: What worked well? What changes should be made for next time?

Social-emotional resiliency and interpersonal skills. Teach learners how to name and manage their emotions. Make interpersonal skills explicit.

Developing your learners' capacities to learn takes intentionality and time, but it is an investment that will pay off. It is important to realize that your students may not have the necessary foundations or grade level skills because of the impact of family circumstances, trauma or other challenges. Design opportunities for learners to develop these skills, which are crucial to life-long learning.

Teaching as a Design Activity

The idea of the study of teaching as a design based activity based upon or science or research is not new and has been considered as an instructional science or design science of instruction (Bruner, 1966; Glaser, 1976; Collins, 1992; Reigeluth, 1978; and Mayer 2003). In recent years, there's been a great deal of research on effective teaching strategies and pedagogical approaches which has resulted in the development of several research-based frameworks for educator use including:

- Robert Marzano's What Works in Classroom Instruction 9 strategies (early 2000's)

- Hattie's Meta-analysis resulting in Visible Learning (2008)

- University of Michigan's High Leverage Teaching Practices (HLTP) (2013)

- American Psychological Association Top 20 Principles for Pre-K to 12 Education (bit.ly/337Zciw)

Each framework presents evidence—or research-based options for strategies and pedagogical approaches that can be used to support impactful instruction. You can think of the strategies and approaches as tools—and different tools are effective for different instructional problems of practice. What good teaching looks like depends quite a bit on the viewer's lens and the discipline from which they are viewing (psychology, cognitive science, sociology, early learning, higher education, etc.). We will explore a range of useful instructional strategies, informed by findings in the learning sciences, later in the chapter.

New Pedagogies for New Literacies: Digital Tools and Technologies

How has technology impacted traditional theories of learning? There are some common ideas about learning that is facilitated, mediated, or framed by digital technologies:

- We are always learning. Learning is not bound by time or place.

- Learning is social and distributed through networks of information.

- Remembering discrete nuggets of factual information is less important now (facts can easily be looked up).

- Learners need guidance in developing skills to effectively categorize, prioritize, and evaluate information (cognitive tasks).

- Digital tools and technologies have and will continue to change the nature of knowledge itself. They will continue to influence the knowledge, skills, and dispositions required to be successful in the 21st-century workplace.

- The idea of new literacies made possible by digital technologies and shaped by social practices in online spaces.

Digital tools and technologies, with their unique affordances (unique capacities or features), have transformed what it means to know, and how we learn. According to How People Learn II (2018), there are eight main affordances of digital technologies that support learning at deeper levels:

1. Interactivity

2. Adaptivity

3. Feedback

4. Choice

5. Non-linear access

6. Linked representations

7. Open-ended learner input

8. Communication with other people

These unique features of digital technologies allow us to learn and teach in completely different ways—impacting the processes and contexts of knowledge acquisition and generation. For example, hyperlinked diagrams or visual representations allow connections to digital media of all types, enabling students to learn through multiple resources and modes. When selecting appropriate digital tools, consider these unique capacities and look for ways to leverage them to achieve learning goals.

Educators have a range of opinions about how digital tools and technologies are important for teaching and for learning. In a course survey, graduate educator learners in Dr. Elkordy's class were asked how technologies impact teaching and learning. They ranked learner agency as being the most impactful concept for teaching with digital technologies (see Figure 4.3). In contrast, the educators viewed engagement as the main advantage of technology for learners (see Figure 4.4).

The rank order of how these practicing teachers, mostly early educators, perceive the applications of technology for instruction may also reflect their own understanding of digital tools and technologies. Educators who are more experienced with using digital tools and technologies for instruction tend to consider more of the unique affordances for particular uses, such as using flipped instruction (extending learning over time and space) or personalized learning (equity of opportunity). For example, providing feedback is rather low on both lists, which suggests opportunities for discussion around this important core practice—using digital tools, feedback can be almost instantaneous which has significant benefits for both educators and learners alike.

How might you respond to these questions? In discussing the use of instructional technologies in our educational teams, it is important to understand colleagues' perceptions. Not sure? Ask!

2. Considering your readings and experience in the classroom, rank the following ways technology impacts teaching, from greatest impact to least:

Item	Overall Rank	Rank Distribution	Score	No. of Rankings
Learner agency ("Learner as owner/driver of own learning")	1		97	14
Use of multiple modes of teaching and learning	2		88	14
Engagement	3		85	14
Motivation	4		71	14
Extension of learning over time and space	5		67	14
Choice	6		62	14
Communication	7		59	14
Learning feedback and assessment	8		56	14

Figure 4.3 | Perceived technology impact on teaching.

10. Considering your readings and experience in the classroom, rank the following ways technology impacts *learning*, from greatest impact to least:

Item	Overall Rank	Rank Distribution	Score	No. of Rankings
Engagement	1		99	14
Motivation	2		99	14
Learner agency ("Learner as owner/driver of own learning")	3		85	14
Choice	4		70	14
Use of multiple modes of teaching and learning	5		69	14
Extension of learning over time and space	6		64	14

Figure 4.4 | Perceived technology impact on learning.

Key Practices for Teaching Digital Age Learners

As educators, a challenging part of our work is knowing when we are making an impact and to what extent. It's almost as if we work to make incremental deposits into our learners' knowledge and skills banks until one day a learner embraces a concept as new understanding and then we know we've made an impact. We use this analogy to share the expectation that the goal is incremental change, which may not be immediately visible. We deposit into the *brain banks* of our learners, nudging them towards understanding and competencies until the skills or knowledge are available for them to retrieve independently—to draw from their own brain bank.

With an incremental multi-faceted approach in mind, we share research-based instructional strategies and associated constructs as viewed through the different approaches, including educational psychology, social psychology, and cognitive sciences. You may see that there is significant overlap in the concepts.

Important Ideas from Educational Psychology

Educational psychology helps us to understand the social, emotional and cognitive processes involved in learning (Mandinach, 2019). It is important for educators to foster student engagement and agency through motivation, choice, self-regulatory skills and metacognition. Neuroscientist-turned-middle-school-teacher, Judy Willis reminds us that learner engagement is critical and that "boredom hurts" (Willis, 2014).

Skills to focus on:

- Metacognition
- Motivation and engagement
- Perseverance / Grit
- Agency
- Self-regulation

Strategies Informed by Cognitive Science

Relevant findings from the cognitive sciences describe thinking and knowledge-building processes. By understanding that our brains seek to novelty because of the way in which information is stored, we can incorporate attention-seeking strategies. Through understanding the idea of schema for cognitive classification, we can understand the need for explicit connections to bridge learning contexts, the impact of cognitive load and the idea of productive struggle (but not beyond learners ZPD).

Strategies to focus on:

- Prior knowledge
- Memory
- Attention
- Retrieval practice
- Explicit connections for transfer of ideas

Table 4.1 presents a sampling of strategies.

Table 4.1 | Strategies Informed by Cognitive Science

STRATEGY	DESCRIPTION	EXAMPLE
Spaced practice	Creating a study or learning schedule that paces activities over time	Study content several times a week instead of once per week.
Interleaving	Periodically switching subjects or content while studying	Prevent study fatigue by alternating subjects.
Retrieval practice	Bringing learned information to mind from long term memory	Use formative quizzes (non-graded), discussions, summarizing, or anything that requires learners to recall learned material.
Elaboration	Asking and explaining context and why things work	Employ questioning, discussions, and role playing
Concrete examples	Provide concrete examples when studying abstract concepts	Share examples of past student work or show application of concepts in real life.
Dual coding	Combining matching words with visuals	Show videos with accompanying closed captions. The images should match the text in content.

(Adapted from Weinstein, Madan, & Sumeracki, 2018)

Improving Teaching Practice through Understanding Impact

Educators naturally reflect upon their practice, building upon successful ideas and trying to troubleshoot issues as they arise in the classroom. In reflection, teachers consider the degree of success—or impact—of their instructional activities. Did we meet our goals? Through experience and implementation of teaching strategies, teachers gain knowledge and expertise in the complex dynamics and pathways of their students' learning. As teachers move through the continuum from novice to expert, they gain expertise which allows them actually to conceive and think differently of instructional problems. It is often very hard for veteran teachers to explain their practice in detail because of the difficulty in remembering what it was like to not know how to approach a problem. For example, classroom organization—remember your first classroom or lab? The specialized knowledge you have since gained—in classroom routines and teaching practices—help you to anticipate and solve problems of practice which once seemed very challenging. Ways of teacher knowing and knowledge seeking are also complex, often depending upon the kind of question. For example, problems of practice are situated or contextualized within specific learning communities with populations of students, parents and learner experiences. The school and classroom cultures play very important roles in determining the norms of behavior and expectations for performance, as do learners' families and social circles.

Why are some teachers successful where others are not? By focusing on individual classrooms, it is easy to overlook solutions that are more big picture in nature. Policy makers, government and funding agencies set well-meaning—but often unfunded—mandates that rarely work to make an impact on student learning that is sustainable and scalable for small and large public schools.

By focusing on improving our teaching practices through studying "what is making the impact?" and by explicitly asking ourselves what factors will enhance our practice and the evidence we weigh in quantifying growth, we can intentionally focus on teacher growth and hence learner achievement. As we design engaging digital learning environments, it's essential to incorporate the best research in the field. We need to examine how we learn, the challenges we face in our learning, and teaching practices that facilitate the learning process for all the students we teach. Through this careful examination, we can begin making impactful changes to practice.

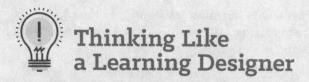

Thinking Like a Learning Designer

The Illiad and Collaborative Learning Challenges

Sara is a new high school English teacher, working in an urban school with a diverse student body. Her first class of the day is a large freshman section which is studying *The Illiad*, Homer's ancient Greek epic about the Trojan War. One strategy that Sara thought could be particularly effective is collaborative learning in small groups. However, she quickly discovered that setting up productive groups was really challenging. As she scanned the room, despite her careful planning to create heterogeneous groups of varied learner abilities, Sara noticed patterns of behavior which were concerning such as unmotivated learners who appeared disinterested or disengaged.

Questions for Reflection

- What kinds of challenges do you think Sara might experience in regards to student motivation? Share possible strategies to improve motivation in her class.

- From a learning design standpoint, why do you think it may be important for Sara to explicitly teach collaboration skills to her students? How could she increase student agency?

- What strategies for improving student motivation would you suggest she try?

- *The Illiad* is a violent tale of the Trojan War. Given that several of her students may have experienced childhood traumas, how might that impact their classroom interactions now? What instructional modifications or strategies would you suggest to Sara?

Chapter Takeaways

- Educators can engage learners to persist in learning tasks by integrating key findings of the learning sciences through teaching strategies and pedagogical approaches.

- Regular reflection upon practice can lead to better teaching and learning.

- Stress, trauma, and instability can affect learners' capacities to form memories and engage in trusting relationships. Special care and attention is needed to build a supportive learning environment.

- Understanding the cognitive task level of your learning activities is key.

- Digital technologies and tools have unique affordances and can leverage our understanding of how learning works.

- Educators can build upon their existing practices by considering the elements of the LITE framework in the context of learning theories when designing instruction. In particular, consideration of the sociocultural context, learner cognition, instructional design, and digital technologies.

Suggested Activities

- As pre-service or early career educators, we are often asked about our Teaching Philosophy as a statement. What's your Learning Philosophy?

- Reflect on your strengths as a teacher. What do you do best in creating impactful learning experiences?

- Ask your students to recall and describe an outstanding, positive learning experience and a negative learning experience. This could be small group work some principles shared. Consider and deconstruct your own practice, in light of students' responses.

- Reflect on when practices are effective and how to use them

- Consider the following focus questions, thinking about both formal and informal learning contexts:

  - How do we know when "learning" has occurred? How can "learning" be effectively measured?

  - What counts as "learning?"

  - How can we leverage assessment and learning progressions for student learning and motivation?

  - How can the use of technologies help or hinder in processes of assessment?

FIELDWORK

Learner Identity

1. How confident are your learners in their abilities to master content? Using learning surveys, ask learners to share their confidence levels on a scale of 1 to 5 (with 5 being the highest) at the beginning—and end of a unit of learning. Share the changes and discuss them with your learners. What did you learn about them? About their needs? About your own practice?

2. Identify three of your own core practices and make goal to increase their effectiveness over a month. Track your progress through journaling—try a bullet journal! (loved by list makers)

3. Evaluate your lesson plans for a week or month, analyzing the cognitive objectives. How often do you ask your students to engage in higher-order thinking? Make a goal to add instructional rigor for deep learning, starting with one activity. Review the learning products with a colleague and ask them to describe the kinds of thinking they see. (Using a Revised Bloom's Taxonomy verb wheel may help, such as the one shown in Figure 4.5 or online at bit.ly/2N0pYUe.)

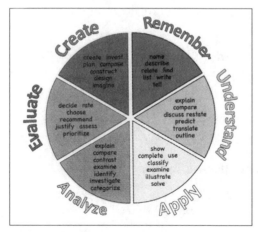

Figure 4.5 | Bloom's Taxonomy wheel.

Learn More: Resources for Further Exploration

Learning Scientists' Ideas of Most Effective Teaching Practices

Deans for Impact: *The science of learning* (bit.ly/2XGOoVj)

Corwin: *Visible learning plus, 250+ influences on student achievement* (bit.ly/2Vu3sDM)

Hattie's 2017 Updated List of Factors Influencing Student Achievement (bit.ly/2F8vCPk)

What Works in Classroom Instruction (bit.ly/2RdDLH0)

The Learning Scientists: *Six Strategies for Effective Learning* (learningscientists.org)

- Videos for Teachers and Students (learningscientists.org/videos)

- Podcasts (learningscientists.org/podcast-episodes)

- Teaching materials (learningscientists.org/downloadable-materials)

Psychologists' Ideas of Most Effective Teaching Practices

American Psychological Association: *Top 20 principles from psychology for preK–12 teaching and learning* (apa.org/ed/schools/teaching-learning/top-twenty-principles.pdf)

American Psychological Association: *Top 20 principles from psychology for prek-12 creative, talented, and gifted students' teaching and learning* (apa.org/ed/schools/teaching-learning/top-principles-gifted.pdf)

American Psychological Association: *Using the top 20 principles* (apa.org/ed/precollege/ptn/2015/09/top-20-principles)

Teacher Educators' Ideas of Most Effective Teaching Practices:

TeachingWorks: *High leverage teaching practices* (teachingworks.org/work-of-teaching/high-leverage-practices)

Turner, S. (2008). Using the Learning Sciences and Knowledge About How People Learn to Support Reluctant and Disengaged Secondary School Learners. *American Secondary Education, 37*(1), 4-16.

Trauma-Informed Schools

Trauma and Learning Policy Initiative (TLPI): *Helping traumatized children learn, Volume 1* (traumasensitiveschools.org/tlpi-publications)

Teachers College Inclusive Classrooms Project (inclusiveclassrooms.org)

Miscellaneous

EdSurge: *I'm a neuroscientist. Here's how teachers change kids' brains* (bit.ly/2If13JU)

The Science Teacher: *Misconceptions and conceptual change in science education* (thescienceteacher.co.uk/misconceptions-in-science-education/)

Empowered Learner: *Neuroscientist is connecting the science of learning to education practice* (bit.ly/2XfrnM8)

Deep Dive

Benassi, V. A., Overson, C. E., & Hakala, C. M. (2014). *Applying science of learning in education: Infusing psychological science into the curriculum.* Retrieved from teachpsych.org/ebooks/asle2014/index.php

Garcia, A., Cantrill, C., Filipiak, D., Hunt, B., Lee, C., Mirra, N., & Peppler, K. (2014). *Teaching in the connected learning classroom.* Irvine, CA: Digital Media and Learning Research Hub.

Hess, K. K. (2012). *Learning progressions in K-8 classrooms: How progress maps can influence classroom practice and perceptions and help teachers make more informed instructional decisions in support of struggling learners* (NCEO Synthesis Report). Retrieved from nceo.umn.edu/docs/OnlinePubs/Synthesis87/SynthesisReport87.pdf

Jones, S. M., Bailey, R., Barnes, S. P., Partee, A., Bailey, R., Barnes, S. P., & Partee, A. (2016). *Executive function mapping project: Untangling the terms and skills related to executive function and self-regulation in early childhood.* Retrieved fromacf.hhs.gov/sites/default/files/opre/ef_mapping_executivesummary_101416_final_508.pdf

Li, N. (2012). Approaches to learning: Literature review. *International Baccalaureate Organization*, 1-34.

National Academies of Sciences, Engineering, and Medicine. (2018). *How people learn II: Learners, contexts, and cultures.* National Academies Press.

Rawson, K. A., Marsh, E. J., Nathan, M. J., & Willingham, D. T. (2013). Improving students' learning with effective learning techniques: Promising directions from cognitive and educational psychology. *Psychological Science in the Public Interest, 14*(1), 4-58.

Retrieval practice website, library, and resources (retrievalpractice.org/library)

Sonia, G. (Ed.). (2017). *Educational research and innovation pedagogical knowledge and the changing nature of the teaching profession.* OECD Publishing. Retrieved from oecd-ilibrary.org/education/pedagogical-knowledge-and-the-changing-nature-of-the-teaching-profession_9789264270695-en

Weinstein, Y., Madan, C. R., & Sumeracki, M. A. (2018). Teaching the science of learning. *Cognitive Research: Principles and Implications, 3*(1), 2.

Willingham, D. T. (2006). How knowledge helps. *American Educator, 30*(1), 30-37.

Willis, J. (2010). The current impact of neuroscience on teaching and learning. *Mind, brain and education: Neuroscience implications for the classroom, 45,* 68.

Willis, J. (2014). Neuroscience reveals that boredom hurts. *Phi Delta Kappan, 95*(8), 28-32.

CHAPTER 5

Understanding Design for Learning

Like pedagogy, design is a term that bridges theory and practice. It encompasses both a principled approach and a set of contextualized practices that are constantly adapting to circumstances. In other words, it is a form of praxis ... in the widely used sense of iterative, reflexive professional learning.

—BEETHAM AND SHARPE, P. 7

This chapter starts by comparing lesson planning to instructional design. It provides an overview of the cycle of design of impactful learning experiences using the LITE framework.

We also explore models and frameworks that help teachers with integrating technology tools into instruction, including Technological Pedagogical Content Knowledge (TPACK), the SAMR model, and the Triple E framework.

By the end of this chapter, you will be able to:

- Explain the rationale and purpose of design for learning

- Apply the design guidelines of the LITE framework to design learning experiences

- Describe how learning progressions and formative assessment work together for individual learning outcomes

- Analyze the cognitive objectives and instructional rationale in applying digital tools and technologies using TPACK and SAMR

- Design learning activities and products using appropriate cognitive objectives

- Explore effective pedagogical approaches for sticky learning

- Explain the impact of learner emotions for learning environments

ISTE Standards Connection

The following standards are addressed in this chapter:

ISTE Standards for Educators

1c. Stay current with research that supports improved student learning outcomes, including findings from the learning sciences.

5c. Explore and apply instructional design principles to create innovative digital learning environments that engage and support learning.

7b. Use technology to design and implement a variety of formative and summative assessments that accommodate learner needs, provide timely feedback to students and inform instruction.

Planning Instruction or Designing for Learning

The typical process of lesson planning is a process of thinking ahead, involving the learning goals or outcomes, lesson content, and activities. There is usually an assessment to determine the extent of student learning.

Depending on the context, the learning targets for a lesson will vary. For example, in PreK through 12 schools, alignment of learning outcomes with state and national standards is very important, and the focus of state and nationwide standardized testing. There are standards, readiness targets, or expectations for every subject and skill, including, scientific knowledge and understanding, English language arts, kindergarten readiness, thinking, mathematics, and social emotional skills.

When it comes to content, many public school systems educators work with established curricula, either purchased as is or designed by the central office of a district. In this case, lesson planning is mostly focused on distributing the curriculum content or chapters of the book in an appropriate manner across the allotted timeframe. The goal is *content coverage*, completing the yearly curriculum map, scope and sequence, or book by the end of the school year. Assessment of learning is usually in the form of summative end-of-chapter or –unit tests, or through standardized testing, which informs the next curriculum delivery cycle, but does little to support student learning in real time as does formative assessment.

It may not be obvious, but when we use these methods of instructional planning, we are making assumptions about the content and materials being used. For example, we may assume that the curriculum is aligned with the latest, most appropriate standards—the same standards upon which the standardized tests are based. We may assume that the materials and instructional strategies are not only research-based but appropriate for every learner—despite how they are unique or different. We may be led to believe that completing a textbook over a year is all that is necessary to meet all the standards for the grade level. But none of these things may be true.

In 2014, Edreports, a nonprofit organization, was formed to review curriculum materials in order to make independent judgements about curriculum publishers' claims of standards alignment. Instructional materials are crucial for K–12 schools, yet surprisingly, Edreports states that "Our analysis shows that only a small fraction

of students (22% in math and 15% in ELA) are exposed to aligned curriculum at least once a week" (Hirsch, 2019). For students in lower-resourced districts, the problem is compounded by the use of older, outdated textbooks. It is entirely possible that students are not taught the curriculum content upon which they are tested. Teachers can check the alignment of their instructional material for English/language arts (K–12), math (K–12), and science (6–8) at edreports.org/reports or by scanning the QR code.

Impactful Designing for Learning

The process of instructional design begins with a deep look at the learning targets, then considers the kinds of learning activities and support materials needed to efficiently and successfully convey the concepts. Assessments are designed to be directly aligned with the learning targets so that the resulting data can be used to determine next instructional steps. Additionally there is a feedback loop that allows for modifications or another period of development.

Instructional design differs from lesson planning in significant ways. Lesson planning typically details the anticipated standards, activities, materials, assessments, and learner accommodation as necessary. While instructional design also requires these elements, the design aspect means attention to specific outcomes—knowledge, skills, and dispositions—and also evidence this was accomplished. Lesson planning may take on the character of the curriculum or textbook to be covered by the end of a unit of time (such as a term or academic year). A learning design informed approach would focus upon the knowledge, skills, and ways of thinking—from a developmental perspective—as the outcomes of instruction over the unit time.

The process of instructional design can be time consuming—particularly for early career educators or teachers who change grade level or subject area. The process requires repeatedly checking alignment with learning targets, activities, and materials and then checking everything with assessment. The payoff, however, is a much higher degree of precision in teaching—with quality instructional designs which may be transferable or effective over different learning contexts. When implemented well, learning design can mean the difference in student understanding and academic performance. Our suggestion is to start small, perhaps with a single goal, and evaluate results. If possible, collaborate with others, such as your grade level team. Once you've experienced the benefits, it's hard to go back to a lesson planning mode!

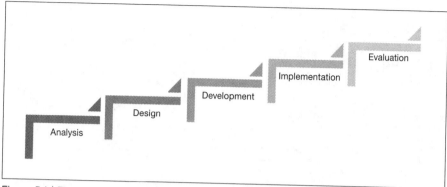

Figure 5.1 | Five phases of the ADDIE model.

There are several well-known models of instructional design, including:

- Gagne's Nine Events of Instruction is a pioneering work that organized the steps of instruction has been highly influential (Gagne & Newell, 1970).

- Understanding by Design is an instructional design model familiar to many educators (Wiggins & McTighe, 2005).

- The Universal Design for Learning (UDL) framework was conceived to provide a baseline of accessibility, for all learners (CAST, 2018).

- The ADDIE model (Figure 5.1) is a systematic instructional design model that includes five phases: analysis, design, development, implementation, and evaluation. The outcome of each phase feeds into the next in the sequence. Components of the ADDIE model are integrated into the Learner and Instruction elements of the LITE model.

The LITE Framework

Consider the LITE framework (Figure 5.2) as a design canvas—essentially a reflection tool to help guide your instructional design process. The LITE framework prompts users to reflect on four areas when designing instruction: learners, instructional strategies and pedagogical approaches, technologies and digital tools, and the environment (context). In thinking through the elements of the framework, consider what do you really want to accomplish in your teaching? For whom? What do your results tell you was accomplished?

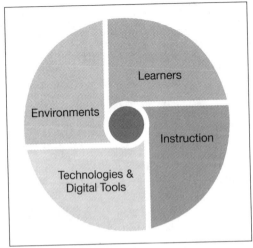

Figure 5.2 | The LITE framework.

Learners

When you consider learners in your design process, first think about their characteristics, capacities, prior knowledge, and readiness for learning. You may want to revisit Chapter 3, where we discussed the types of learner characteristics and capacities that impact learning. While there is no evidence to support the use of learning styles for more effective learning, learners do have preferences about learning modalities. Leveraging learner preferences can help with motivation and engagement as well as influence the degree to which they enjoy using the various tools and kinds of instructional strategies or projects.

Student beliefs about their own abilities to accomplish tasks (self-efficacy) and teacher expectations of students are highly impactful on student learning. According to John Hattie's meta-analysis of factors impacting instruction, teachers' and students' estimates of achievement and self-reported estimates respectively, are among the most impactful strategies in learning (Hattie, 2017). Furthermore, the recently updated study found that collective teacher efficacy, the "collective belief of teachers in their ability to positively affect students," is *the* most impactful influence on student achievement! (Hattie, 2017)

Engaging students in meaningful relationships has always been important for educators—but it's not until recently that we have evidence of how much this influence of educators on their learners has an impact—particularly for the higher-needs students. One of the most important benefits of positive relationships is the trust your learners have in you as their teacher—and their willingness to reach out to you when experiencing challenges. If you'd like to learn more about how your learners approach learning, their likes and dislikes, try giving them short, simple surveys or polls using Google forms or other digital tools. Students love to participate and often share useful information that can help in designing more effective instruction. Dr. Elkordy's students create short surveys for their own students as part of creating learner profiles. Her graduate teacher-learners are always surprised at their findings!

Instruction

As educators, we must leverage our knowledge of how students learn by building upon existing schema. As a reminder, think of schema as the brain's tools for classification and sorting. To effectively connect new knowledge with the existing knowledge or schema, it is essential to activate students' prior knowledge. We bring out prior learning by asking our learners to retrieve the information from their memories, which is why this aspect of instruction is so important.

To discover your learners' understanding, then plan instruction to build upon that knowledge, it's important to carefully assess it before beginning instruction. Understanding the extent—and possible deficits—of learners' existing knowledge is essential to deciding which pedagogical approaches and instructional methods would be best for the targeted learning outcomes. This assessment will also help you to uncover any possible misconceptions, which are important to correct before proceeding. If the foundation, the existing schema, is incorrect, then the new knowledge will also be riddled with misunderstanding.

Learning Progressions

For learning that is deep, enduring, and memorable—that is, *sticky* learning—it is important for educators to understand how learners conceptualize ideas in order to be able to address gaps between expected and actual performance on tasks. In order to effectively differentiate and assess understanding of individual learning gaps,

> teachers need to have in mind a continuum of how learning develops in any particular knowledge domain so that they are able to locate students' current learning status and decide on pedagogical action to move students' learning forward. Learning progressions that clearly articulate a progression of learning in a domain can provide the big picture of what is to be

learned, support instructional planning, and act as a touchstone for forma-tive assessment. (Heritage, 2008, p. 2)

A learning continuum or trajectory, specifies a sequence of distinct skills or bodies of knowledge in which learners must prove proficiency before moving on to the next set of skills. Such learning progressions generally articulate typical paths for building knowledge in a domain at a detailed level.

In the classroom, educators have specific goals for instruction, and target outcomes that are often aligned with state and/or national standards, such as the CCSS or NGSS. Each of the standards, in turn, involves several skills and bodies of enabling knowledge that learners must master to be considered *proficient* in the knowledge represented by the standard. As a set of targets or benchmarks, educational stan-dards could be considered an outline or scaffold of required knowledge and skills.

Learning progressions differ from descriptions of chunks of knowledge typically represented in curriculum maps or scope and sequences in that they incorporate the premise of a continuum though which learners may progress from novice to expert, instead of learners demonstrating proficiency in discrete skills or competen-cies (Heritage, 2008). Consider standards as having *recipes* for success—and we know how much outcomes can vary from the same recipe!

If we consider the idea of learning progressions as continuous (although not necessarily sequential) growth in domain-based knowledge, we can understand how challenging it would be to list every single discrete chunk of information needed for in-depth understanding.

Formative Assessments

Strategically designed and implemented formative assessments can be effective in uncovering learners' gaps in prior knowledge, misconceptions, or misunderstanding of learning strategies—all of which must be addressed for constructing new, sticky knowledge. While an in-depth discussion of formative assessments is beyond the scope of this book, it is important for educators to understand the role of learning targets, evidence of success, and instructional modifications to address perfor-mance gaps.

Summative assessments are used primarily for grading or macro-educational deci-sions—is the learner on track? Yes or no. Formative assessments embedded within instruction, however, can be implemented at multiple, key points in the learning progression so that instructional corrections can be made in a timely manner.

Knowing which chunks of knowledge are the most important is a matter of pedagogical content knowledge, the specialized expertise teachers develop through practice. Take for example, your carefully thought-out lesson on water ecosystems and insects, taught in a suburban context, which resulted in a range of learner performance. Looking at the data, you notice that the struggling learners are from urban contexts and have never seen small-scale freshwater systems such as ponds or lakes. This represents a disadvantage.

In designing learning experiences, it is critical to keep the instructional goals or learning targets in mind, as well as evidence of successful attainment of the goals or desired learner outcomes. The learning activities should be aligned with, and assessed at, the appropriate cognitive level, and be mindful of domain or content level learning progressions. Teachers can help the transfer of important concepts within or across domains by making explicit connections—through strategies such as deep questioning, analogy, or visual representations.

While the need for alignment between activities and learning objectives is clear, alignment with the assessment or demonstration of learning is key also. Consider what kinds of skills and knowledge are actually being reinforced or assessed through rubrics or grading. Think about a common assignment for elementary students: to create posters or presentations. The grading criteria specifies including three facts, three pictures, and a particular size of poster board. What skills are being reinforced? Older students are asked to prepare presentations on topics which share declarative or lower-order thinking. What skills are being reinforced here? The use of tools such as Bloom's revised taxonomy can help to determine the cognitive levels of tasks we ask of our learners. When assigning cognitive levels, it is important to know if learners have the appropriate prior knowledge.

Understanding Cognitive Tasks: Bloom's (Revised) Taxonomy

Blooms' Taxonomy refers to Benjamin Bloom's work centering on educational learning objectives. The highly influential classification scheme was first developed by a committee of educators, led by Bloom, at the University of Chicago in 1956. Its purpose is to define and distinguish different levels of human cognition. Bloom's framework has been applied by generations of educators, both PK–12 and college instructors, to identify the level of learning and cognitive processes. The learning outcomes are arranged into six categories: Knowledge, Comprehension, Application, Analysis, Synthesis, and Evaluation. These six categories were developed on a continuum from elementary (knowledge) to complex (evaluation) and from concrete to abstract skills and abilities. In the original taxonomy, content knowledge was presented as the mandatory precondition for putting these skills and talents into practice.

In 2001, Anderson & Krathwohl published a revision of the taxonomy, which remains widely used. The nouns of the original taxonomy were replaced by action verbs that describe the cognitive processes by which learners think and learn. The familiar yet slightly different categories are, in order from simple to complex: Remember, Understand, Apply, Analyze, Evaluate, and Create. The revised taxonomy "provides a clear, concise visual representation" (Krathwohl, 2002) of the alignment between standards and educational goals, objectives, products, and activities. Educators use Bloom's revised taxonomy to plan instructional activities and to differentiate lower- and higher-order thinking skills.

Technologies and Digital Tools

In considering our students' learning, it's important to remember that they are learning both in and out of school. Now that students are essentially empowered to look up facts, information, or declarative knowledge, there's less of an emphasis on remembering large amounts of information but rather the knowledge of how and where to find it. Digital media, tools, and websites empower learners to easily connect with resources and independent interests. Self-directed learning and networks are a crucial part of learning and so thinking of students' learning activities holistically instead of only academic learning is key.

Imagine, for example, that as a learner at home you can independently research your interests and connect with others, perhaps experts and like-minded friends. When you attend school, however, mobile devices may be banned and your learning tasks are memorization of seemingly disconnected facts with few applications. The connected learning framework, proposed by researcher Mimi Ito and colleagues Gutierrez, Livingston, Penuel, Salen, and Watkins (2013), describes core principles and contexts which build upon and extend existing theories of learning into the digital realm:

- Peer supported
- Interest-powered
- Academically oriented
- Production centered
- Shared purpose and
- Openly networked

The framework integrates key aspects of social constructivist learning principles (learning is social and essentially occurs through interaction with others' ideas) with the increased capacity for self-motivated learning through digital tools and technologies—anytime and anywhere. A key goal of education is to create independent, life-long learners. Inviting learners, when appropriate, to bring in their knowledge from outside of school values all learning, regardless of context. For the learner, this will result in a smaller division between in and out-of-school learning when both *count*.

The implementation of digital tools and technologies for instruction and pedagogies goes far beyond the frequently cited student engagement. From a practical perspective, our learning changes our brains—and this also means that frequent technology use changes our brain structures. For example, Mayer (2005), proposed cognitive principles of multimedia learning including: dual auditory and visual processing channels for processing information, limited capacity, and active processing (filtering, selecting, organizing, and integrating information). His principles describe the active role of cognition in processing and sense making of incoming perceptual data. His findings on how learners process multimedia information—written words, pictorial representations, and audio—are useful in the preparation of learning materials.

For many educators, student engagement is the primary goal of using digital tools and technologies for teaching. Understanding the possibilities of technology enhanced instruction, however, means knowledge of how to use technologies' unique properties for instruction and learning. For the appropriate use of digital technologies to support instructional objectives, educators must be able to gauge the level of cognitive tasks. They must then determine how to meaningfully integrate the use of digital tools as essential and integral to the tasks—not as inconsequential add-ons.

Mishra and Koehler's model, Technological Pedagogical Content Knowledge or TPACK (2006), was a pioneer in describing the kind of specialized knowledge that educators need to effectively use digital tools and technologies in instruction. The TPACK framework advances the idea that teachers develop knowledge about how and when to use digital tools and technologies to support their pedagogical approach. There are several useful frameworks and tools that have been developed to assist educators in assessing the cognitive level of tasks, such as Bloom's Digital Taxonomy (Churches, 2008); and in evaluating the level or type of application, such as the SAMR (Puentedura, 2010) or Triple E frameworks (Kolb, 2017). Applying these frameworks can help educators to use digital technologies in effective ways when designing instruction.

TPACK

The TPACK concept—sometimes referred to as TPCK—builds upon the construct of pedagogical content knowledge (PCK), the specialized expertise educators build about instruction that is learned through reflection upon instructional practices. Novice teachers develop PCK through experience, for example, teaching fractions while being mindful of typical learner questions or errors, or being explicit about the idea of some systems in nature as being analogous to systems of government. Expertise in pedagogical approaches and instructional strategies increases over time—it's the *how* of the teaching. TPACK is the distinctive knowledge of effective technology-use practices to achieve instructional objectives—using the best tools for the desired learner outcomes. For more about TPACK, see the Learn More resources at the end of the chapter.

SAMR Model

In 2010, Ruben Puentendra proposed the Substitution, Augmentation, Modification, or Redefinition (SAMR) model, which proposes four degrees of technology integration. The SAMR model provides a common language or framework to use when considering technology use when designing instruction. At the substitution level, there is a low level of usage of digital tools. For example, learners may type a story instead of writing by hand. Using this example, augmentation could mean learners publish their work digitally and seek peer feedback. The modification level could entail creating a document containing digital media, and redefinition could mean creating a hyperlinked document as a blog, published for a peer, globally-situated audience. Educators can use the scale to build expertise, metacognition and TPACK as they self-evaluate their technology use.

Triple E framework

Perhaps the most teacher-friendly framework, the Triple E framework, was developed by teacher educator Dr. Liz Kolb and colleagues at the University of Michigan (2017). Teachers appreciate the framework's ease of use, clarity, and ongoing professional development support by ISTE through webinars, twitter chats, and book studies. The Triple E framework and accompanying rubric assists educators in evaluating the role of digital tools and technologies to—Engage, Enhance, or Extend learning.

Bloom's Digital Taxonomy

Bloom's Taxonomy is an important tool that learning designers can use to evaluate and assign tasks of appropriate cognitive levels to attain learner outcomes.

The revised taxonomy features verb wheels which align verbs with the six cognitive levels—great tools to design individual or sequences of learning tasks. They are also helpful in deconstructing standards into their respective skills.

TEACHERS THINK: TPACK AND SAMR

Both TPACK and SAMR are similar in the sense that they both include how technology is incorporated into teaching and learning. They both look at how technology can be used to enhance students understanding and the way they learn. However, TPACK is more of a guide that encourages the use of pedagogy and content knowledge while incorporating technology. The SAMR model looks at how to redefine instruction with technology. It does not highlight the idea that teachers are using their knowledge of both content and pedagogy to support learning and picking the best technology to fit or support students.

I would want to share the TPACK model with our staff and district. I feel that this model is a more positive way to look at technology integration, looking at the experiences and knowledge teachers bring to the table. This would also show them that technology would just be improving or enhancing what they already do.

—KELLY FUNK, TEACHER

In 2008, Educator Andrew Churches updated Bloom's original taxonomy to include new applications based on the unique affordances and context when using digital tools and technologies. According to Churches, "Bloom's revised taxonomy describes many traditional classroom practices, behaviors and actions, but does not account for the new processes and actions associated with Web 2.0 technologies" (Edorigami wiki, 2008).

One major difference in the digital taxonomy is how Churches shows the progression of skills from LOTS (lower-order thinking skills) to HOTS (higher-order thinking skills). The verbs in the digital taxonomy apply to technology use in the digital 21st century classroom. Churches goes on to explain that the revised taxonomy "is an update which attempts to account for the new behaviors and actions emerging as technology advances and becomes more ubiquitous" (2008).

Explore Bloom's digital taxonomy and other great resources in the Learn More section at the end of the chapter.

Environments

Learning is situated within an environment or a context, which means that our memories of learning are intermingled with memories of how and where we learned. This environment can include many factors and be quite complex, so it's helpful to take a big picture view of the most impactful factors. In the brain-targeted teaching model, former-teacher-turned-professor Dr. Mariale Hardiman of Johns Hopkins University, introduces six brain targets, with the first two devoted to building the environment. The six brain targets are:

1. Establishing the emotional climate for learning

2. Creating the physical learning environment

3. Designing the learning experience

4. Teaching for mastery of content, skills, and concepts

5. Teaching for the extension and application of knowledge

6. Evaluating learning (2012)

Hardiman's principles apply to creating learning environments for learners of any age; for example, it is as important for adults as it is for middle schoolers to create a safe emotional climate when learners are experiencing the vulnerability inherent in learning new skills. While the means and context may vary widely—online learning, the school playground, gym, 4th grade classroom, or professional development workshop—establishing a context of care and acceptance is crucial.

Hardiman also encourages attention to the small details of the physical environment that teachers may be intuitively addressing, such as hanging instructional materials and work in the classroom. By adding features that are informed and supported by neuroscience findings, teachers can intentionally design the environment to influence student learning. For example, teachers can leverage the powerful understanding that learners' brains seek out stimulation and change by simply making the classroom look different. According to Hardiman, "Novelty in the environment triggers the alerting and orienting systems. Unchanging visual environments create habituation (p. 61)." Habituation means that a stimulus has been around for a while and is no longer interesting—or stimulating—and if learners don't pay attention to materials, they won't learn from them.

The message in Hardiman's work and others is that learning contexts should be considered as self-sustaining, interdependent ecosystems that can and should be designed. This view is empowering for educators who eagerly embrace simple ideas such as adding small meditation routines, green plants, or small amounts of essential oils to promote productive states of relaxed awareness for learners.

Considering the learning context can also mean considering how content is presented. For example, arts integration may improve long term content retention (Rinne, Gregory, Yarmolinskaya, & Hardiman, 2011).

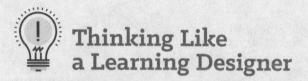

Thinking Like a Learning Designer

The Learning Environment

Reflect on the environment of your teaching context. How do you shape the culture in your teaching, or does it just happen? What student-centered strategies could you use to promote a positive culture? To deflect negativity? Think deeply about the implications of your knowledge of the learning environment and your capacity to design the learner experience. Suggest two small strategies you could begin to implement and assess their impact on the instructional environment.

Chapter Takeaways

- Learning design increases the reliability and effectiveness of learner outcomes.

- Educators should be aware of major milestones or benchmarks in learning progressions, for example, walking before running or understanding place value before double-digit multiplication.

- Learning progressions represent a holistic view of learning in a domain, instead of discrete skills and bodies of knowledge which are not connected.

- By using formative assessment strategies and knowledge of learning progressions, teachers can be more precise in their practice.

- Bloom's Taxonomy and its various revisions and digital tools are useful when designing instructional activities for specific cognitive objectives.

- Technological-pedagogical content knowledge (TPACK) is the specialized knowledge teachers develop to successfully implement instructional technologies.

- The SAMR framework is a tool used to assess the current level of technology-based instruction and to design enhancements.

- The Triple E framework is a user-friendly and helpful set of teaching tools for designing impactful, technology-based activities for student engagement, instructional enhancement, and extension.

- Educators can examine their own practice—by reviewing assessment data, conducting action research, or collaborating in other engaged research methodologies such as design-based research.

- A thoughtfully designed and implemented system for motivation and scaffolding of learning, such as digital badges, can be effective for developing learner metacognition, motivation, and persistence-at-task—all important qualities for independent, life-long learning.

- Educators should consider the impact of learner emotions, classroom layout, and environmental aspects for learning.

Suggested Activities

1. **Conceptualization of Learning:** As an educator, you may have shared your visions of good teaching practices through a teaching philosophy or statement. How would you conceptualize your understanding of how learning happens for your learners? Share your conceptualization through a learning statement, taking care to describe how knowledge is built for individuals.

2. **Learner Surveys:** Educators intuitively understand the importance of good relationships with their learners—as well as respect for individual differences. Many of us, however, have never collected learner opinions on a broad basis. Short learning surveys are a great way to accomplish this. Using a platform such as Google forms, educators can ask about the processes and perceptions—learners' experiences in their class or environment. While learning surveys are a kind of formative assessment, they are designed to elicit information about the learner experience and behaviors instead of learner understanding of a topic.

Typical questions may ask about learner preferences and ask learners to evaluate their own learning, for example:

- How do you learn best?

- Reflect upon and describe your problem solving strategy for x.

- What role (e.g., leader, recorder, time-keeper) do you usually play in group work and why? Describe the roles.

- On a scale of 1 to 5, with 5 being the highest score, rate your effort on x project, assignment, or activity. What grade/score should you receive? Explain your answers.

- What are your biggest challenges in completing homework?

- What do you do when you are stuck on a math problem? Why?

- What motivates you to continue working when the task is difficult?

- On a scale of 1 to 5, with 5 being the highest score, rate your confidence in x subject/content. (This is a good pre- and post-in-struction question.)

- Is there anything you think I should know about your work?

Not only does surveying your learners help you gather actionable information for instruction, it incorporates several high leverage practices such as engaging learners in reflecting and rating their own learning and developing learners' metacognition. Sharing data with your learners on a particular project, assignment, or activity will help them to develop data literacy and metacognition and potentially ease performance anxiety. Learners will appreciate the dialogue about their learning, which demonstrates a level of care and interest that leads to strong relationships.

Dr. Elkordy shares aggregated course data anonymously through visuals such as pie charts or bar graphs. Write-in answers, particularly when learners are sharing personal information, are not shared. Open-ended responses to questions such as "What are your top three takeways from this lesson?" may be shared, but learners are always alerted when their responses will be shared with others.

Try it yourself! Create a short survey of 4–5 questions using Google forms (or start with a paper form). The results are always surprising!

FIELDWORK

Surveying the Learning Landscape

1. **Learning Environment Observation:** Prepare a checklist of 10–15 items for an observer conducting a *walk-through* in an academic/formal setting. Select a role and learning context, such as the ones listed below:

   - School administrator (principal/teacher leader) at brick and mortar school

   - School administrator (principal/teacher leader) at online school

   - Director of training (adult education)

   - Director of digital learning in museum or library (specify)

   - After-school program coordinator

   - Parent or guardian

   - Prospective student

   You may specify circumstances—for example: I'm a principal of a K–5 charter school focusing on STEM.

   What components are visible in a productive learning environment from your lens? What would you expect to see?

2. **Learner Landscape Study:** The goal of this study is to understand how learner affect, motivation, and strategies change in different learning contexts, as well as how characteristics such as motivation and persistence change.

   - Select one or two students to study, comparing and contrasting their learning behaviors in different contexts to get a "360°" view. How do they learn in different environments? Select students who are active in extracurricular activities or self-directed learning.

   - Investigate patterns of learning in 2 or 3 different learning contexts. In different activities, observe the level and kind of motivation. What happens when learning is hard? (Consider persistence-at-task—do they give up or push through?)

- Compare and contrast learner behaviors in the different contexts. What did you observe?

3. **Learner Profile:** Survey a group of learners within the same grade band or age group about how they use technology to learn, both in-school and out, in order to understand how they approach the learning environment. Use Google forms or paper surveys to construct a short survey and collect the data. Ask students about their learning habits, interest, and persistence at task in appropriate-level language. Analyze your data by comparing and contrasting learner strategies, approach, and characteristics; either individually or as a synthesis.

Learn More:
Resources for Further Exploration

Examples of Educational Standards

Collaborative for Academic, Social, and Emotional Learning (CASEL) tools for developing Social-emotional standards (drc.casel.org/standards)

Common Core State Standards (CCSS) (corestandards.org)

ISTE Standards for Students (iste.org/standards/for-students)

Next Generation Science Standards (NGSS) (nextgenscience.org)

Instructional Design

ADDIE model (instructionaldesign.org/models/addie)

Educational Origami: *Bloom's Activity Analysis Tool* (bit.ly/2MXY9xg)

Dr. Mariale Hardiman, Johns Hopkins University: *Brain-Targeted Teaching* (braintargetedteaching.org)

Byrdseed: *The Differentiator* [tool based on Bloom's Taxonomy, Kaplan and Gould's Depth and Complexity, and David Chung's product menu] (byrdseed.com/differentiator)

Diana Laurillard: *Learning Designer* [tool based on the six learning types from Diana Laurillard's Conversational Framework] (ucl.ac.uk/learning-designer)

Arizona State University: *Learning Objectives Builder* [tool for creating measurable course outcomes and learning objectives] (teachonline.asu.edu/objectives-builder)

Gagne's nine events of instruction (bit.ly/2KhTDrv)

Judy Dirksen: Design for how people learn [video] (youtu.be/-0BRVg3mHk4)

CAST: *UDL and the Learning Brain* (bit.ly/2WKSKOC)

Common Sense Education: *SAMR and Bloom's Taxonomy: Assembling the Puzzle* (bit.ly/2H3JU4P)

Digital Promise: *Powerful Learning is Personal and Accessible* (bit.ly/2F6EFAb)

Tools to Gauge the Level of Digital Technology Usage

Kathy Schrock's Bloomin Apps including resources aligned to Bloom's Taxonomy (schrockguide.net/bloomin-apps.html)

The TPACK Framework Explained (with Classroom Examples) (schoology.com/blog/tpack-framework-explained)

Triple E framework (tripleeframework.com)

SAMR and Bloom's (schrockguide.net/samr.html)

Emerging Edtech: *8 Examples of Transforming Lessons through the SAMR Cycle* (bit.ly/2KR1rQg)

Deep Dive

Carr-Chellman, A. A. (2015). *Instructional design for teachers: Improving classroom practice*. Routledge.

Connected Learning Alliance. (2018). *Connected learning explained*. Retrieved from clalliance.org/resources/connected-learning-explained

Dirksen, J. (2016). *Design for how people learn*. Pearson

Elkordy, A. (2013). InfoMaker badge series level 1 (goo.gl/zdgevK)

Hess, K. K. (2010). Using learning progressions to monitor progress across grades. *Science and Children, 47*(6), 57.

Hess, K. K. (2012). *Learning progressions in k-8 classrooms: How progress maps can influence classroom practice and perceptions and help teachers make more informed instructional decisions in support of struggling learners* (NCEO Synthesis Report). Retrieved from conservancy.umn.edu/bitstream/handle/11299/173798/SynthesisReport87. pdf?sequence=1

Mayer, R. E. (2005). Cognitive theory of multimedia learning. *The Cambridge handbook of multimedia learning, 43.*

Puentedura, R. (2010). *SAMR and TPCK: Intro to advanced practice.* Retrieved from http://hippasus.com/resources/sweden2010/SAMR_TPCK_ IntroToAdvancedPractice.pdf

Popham, W. J. (2007). The lowdown on learning progressions. *Educational Leadership, 64*(7), 83.

PART II

·················

Designing Powerful
Learning Experiences

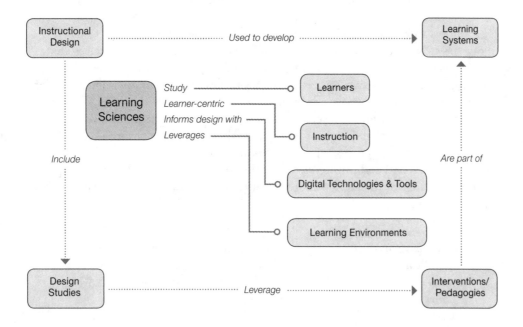

THIS SECTION:

- introduces the reader to the design process, with a focus on learners' experience

- explores the 4C's—critical thinking, communication, collaboration, and creativity—through the LITE framework to inform design of learning for skill development

- informs the creation of designed or engineered experiences through the four components of the LITE model—Learners, Instruction, Digital Technologies & Tools, and Learning Environments

Generally, educators in the teacher preparation context aren't introduced to the idea of instruction being cycles, or asked to consider their work situated within systems. The complexity of teaching requires time, practice, and reflection to be effective—and in a real sense, these views resonate more with practicing teachers. As you gain expertise in a few highly effective practices, it is possible to consider these wider perspectives. The core of instructional design is teacher presence—the decisions you make to support clear learning objectives.

We adopt this view as we apply the LITE framework for learning design to the 4C's: critical thinking, communication, collaboration, and creativity. Despite their importance, many teachers aren't specifically taught how or what to teach about the 4C's. Like educational standards, educators often find themselves alone when considering the meaning and instructional implications. What is critical thinking? What is creativity? What do collaboration and communication mean for 21st-century learners? What kinds of new literacies, such as or data literacies, have developed due to technological change in our world—and what should we teach our learners? It is probably not surprising that there is a range of interpretations of these concepts. The process of design requires us to deeply consider the learning outcomes—intended and unintended—clearly. Designing powerful learning experiences is critical as educators work together to prepare learners for the rapidly changing world.

> *[W]e have to rethink how we do school. 'There are systems we've created for efficiency, not to get people to learn things," [Sir Ken] Robinson stated, later adding, "We organize our kids' learning by their date of birth. We don't do that anywhere else, except school."*
>
> —MADDA, 2017

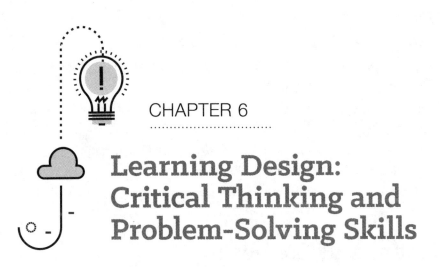

CHAPTER 6

Learning Design: Critical Thinking and Problem-Solving Skills

We all endorse it and we all want our students to do it. We also claim to teach it. "It" is critical thinking, and very few of us actually teach it or even understand what it is.

—PAUL & ELDER, 2013; NILSON, 2018

This chapter explores one of the 4C's, critical thinking, and associated problem-solving skills. We discuss the importance and forms of critical thinking as well as the design of learning experiences to promote these skills for digital age learners.

By the end of this chapter, you will be able to:

- Explain critical thinking and its importance for learners

- Describe instructional strategies to promote critical thinking, including questioning, brainstorming, and inquiry

- Design learning experiences and environments to foster the development of critical thinking skills using the LITE framework

- Explore effective strategies to promote critical thinking in a range of learning contexts and purposes using digital tools and technologies

- Promote a culture of critical thinking in the learning environment

ISTE Standards Connection

The following standards are addressed in this chapter:

ISTE Standards for Students

3. Knowledge Constructor. Students critically curate a variety of resources using digital tools to construct knowledge, produce creative artifacts and make meaningful learning experiences for themselves and others.

ISTE Standards for Educators

5. Designer. Educators design authentic, learner-driven activities and environments that recognize and accommodate learner variability.

ISTE Standards for Coaches

2. Teaching, Learning, and Assessments. Technology Coaches assist teachers in using technology effectively for assessing student learning, differentiating instruction, and providing rigorous, relevant, and encouraging learning experiences for all students.

> **2d.** Coach teachers in and model design and implementation of technology-enhanced learning experiences emphasizing creativity, higher order thinking skills and processes, and mental habits of mind (e.g., critical thinking, metacognition, and self-regulation).

ISTE Standards for Education Leaders

Connected Leader 5c. Education leaders use technology to regularly engage in reflective practices that support personal and professional growth.

Critical Thinking

Critical thinking is a set of cognitive skills that are applied purposefully (learner-directed) to make decisions, solve problems, and weigh evidence. Critical thinking also refers to ways of thinking learners need to develop to become lifelong learners, informed participants in a democratic society, and both critical consumers as well as producers of information in our world of digitally-constructed and distributed knowledge. In an age of information overwhelm, understanding how to reason and evaluate using evidence are essential skills.

While educators are charged with teaching their learners how to think critically, there is a lack of understanding or clear definition of how this may differ among disciplines, for example, critical thinking in language arts or science, which complicates teaching these essential skills. In an article about teaching in higher education, Linda Nilson (2018) contends, "It is little wonder we don't understand what critical thinking is. The literature around it is abstract and fragmented among several different scholars or scholarly teams who work in their own silos and don't build on or even cite each other." As a result, you will probably encounter many different definitions of critical thinking.

The introduction of critical thinking into education began with John Dewey (1910), who called it "reflective thinking" (p. 118). He defined reflective thinking as "active, persistent, and careful consideration of any belief or supposed form of knowledge in the light of the grounds that support it, and the further conclusions to which it tends" (Dewey 1910, p. 6; 1933, p. 9).

Psychologist and educator Diane Halpern (1996) articulated a practical definition for educators working with K–12 learners:

> Critical thinking uses evidence and reason. It is thinking that is purposeful, reasoned, and goal-directed—the kind of thinking involved in solving problems, formulating inferences, calculating likelihoods, and making decisions, when the thinker is using skills that are thoughtful and effective for the particular context and type of thinking task. (p. 8)

Critical thinking is sometimes called directed thinking because it focuses on a desired outcome (Halpern, 1996). It is this careful and goal-directed thinking that we want to develop in all our learners focusing on a desired outcome. From the standpoint of cognitive science, what we refer to as critical thinking is usually one of three different kinds of thinking: reasoning, evaluating (making judgments and decisions), and problem-solving (Willingham, 2007). As a construct—a definition of an abstract concept—we don't see critical thinking as it is happening but must infer it from evidence.

Educators must recognize the kinds of learning products that effectively demonstrate evidence of critical thinking. As we consider critical thinking and problem-solving skills and how they may manifest or look in our learning contexts, it is important to think about the most impactful strategies to develop critical thinking skills for all diverse learners. Critical thinking occurs when students are analyzing, evaluating, interpreting, or synthesizing information and applying creative thought to form an argument, solve a problem, or reach a conclusion. In turn, educators need effective instructional strategies and pedagogical approaches—as well as the ability to recognize, measure, and promote critical thinking skills.

Broadbear (2003) suggested specific strategies that teachers could integrate into their instruction to promote the development of critical thinking, including using criteria such as clarity, logic, relevance, and accuracy to assess learner thinking; and using ill-structured problems. Ill-structured problems do not have single solutions, nor can the problem be fully defined—there are consequences for every solution and in thinking these through, learners will develop and enhance their critical thinking skills.

Citing research from Paul & Elder (2013), Nilson says that although we claim to understand critical thinking—and teach it—in reality, it is not consistently taught by higher education faculty. In their study of over 50 universities, Paul, Elder, & Bartell (1997) found:

- Though the overwhelming majority (89%) claimed critical thinking to be a primary objective of their instruction, only a small minority (19%) could give a clear explanation of what critical thinking is.

- Although the vast majority (89%) stated that critical thinking was of primary importance to their instruction, 77% of the respondents had little, limited, or no conception of how to reconcile content coverage with the fostering of critical thinking.

If critical thinking is valued—but not consistently taught in educator preparation and other higher education programs—it's no surprise that the uncertainty and confusion carry over to educators working in K–12 learning contexts.

Critical thinking skills, crucial for the economy, democracy, governance, and productive lives for our learners, should be promoted in schools. Graduates of our educational institutions "need a conceptual understanding of complex concepts, and the ability to work with them creatively to generate new ideas, new theories, new products, and new knowledge. They need to be able to critically evaluate what they read" (OECD, p. 1).

Design for Critical Thinking: The LITE Framework

What are the essential conditions for promoting critical thinking and problem-solving skills? We will discuss the four elements of the LITE framework (Figure 6.1)—learners, instructional strategies and pedagogical approaches, technology and digital tools, and environment—in terms of the learning design for promoting strong critical thinking and problem-solving skills for all learners.

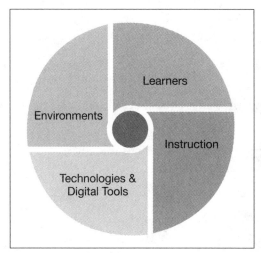

Figure 6.1 | The LITE framework.

Learners

Students need to have many critical thinking skills in their brain bank, especially in the areas of metacognition, self-regulation, self-efficacy, and flexible thinking. Figure 6.2 identifies skills and dispositions that foster critical thinking.

The folllowing list explains and expands the list of critical thinking skills.

- Reasoning: the ability to examine and provide evidence when decision making

- Analysis: the ability to deconstruct a situation or problem into its component parts to identify the sources

- Evaluation: the ability to prioritize key points and compare to outcomes

- Synthesis: the ability to combine ideas, knowledge, processes or procedures

- Inferencing: the ability to make a reasonable prediction or extrapolation based upon evidence

- Problem-solving skills

- Ability to effectively engage in dialog with others

- Creating an argument or position to support a claim from evidence

- Ideas transfer: the ability to transfer ideas into new contexts

- Making connections: the ability to make connections between existing knowledge and new applications

- Ability to deconstruct a problem into its components

To develop students' critical thinking skills, teachers should design activities that help students:

- apply age-appropriate higher-order thinking skills such as analysis, inference, evaluation, and/or synthesis

- be flexible thinkers who consider a variety of perspectives

- develop curiosity for new ideas and insights

- recognize the importance of being well-informed when decision making

- seek and identify evidence to support a claim or argument

- articulate the processes of their own thinking (metacognition)

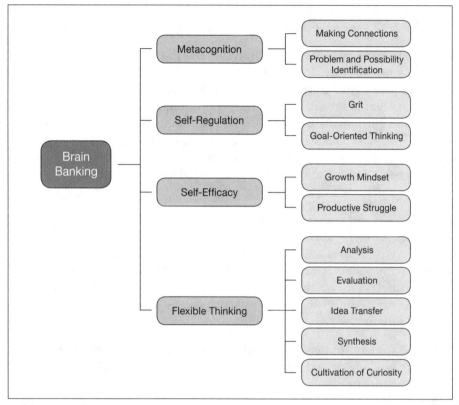

Figure 6.2 | Skills that foster critical thinking.

- understand the difference between things happening together and one thing being the cause of another (correlation versus causation)

- demonstrate a willingness to seek and consider the opinions of others

- develop domain-level knowledge

- exhibit curiosity and willingness to take intellectual risks

Instructional Strategies and Pedagogical Approaches

Learners are routinely curious or thoughtful, particularly when the content is personally interesting; but this doesn't necessarily mean they are critical thinkers. These skills—or habits of mind—are acquired or developed capacities. "Critical thinking is not an innate ability. Although some students may be naturally inquisitive, they require training to become systematically analytical, fair, and open-minded in their pursuit of knowledge" (Snyder & Snyder, 2008, p. 92).

Essential strategies to promote critical thinking and problem-solving skills require learners to use higher-order thinking skills such as questioning, brainstorming, inquiry- or problem-based learning, as well as reflection to build metacognition. Educators can also use *thinking routines*, the deliberate application of different kinds of thinking in a small, memorable series. Thinking routines are like *heuristics*, routines that follow specific steps depending upon the type of problem encountered. The ability to think critically is intertwined with the subject or content—what essentially is being thought about—so knowledge and understanding are key. (Willingham, 2007).

Have you ever observed your learners struggling with new questions or problems that resemble ones you've already covered in your curriculum and wondered why? Learners need explicit connections between content and problem-solving strategies—this could include clarification (e.g., "This is a fraction problem") or using thinking routines, which make thinking—and learning—visible. It's also important to permit learners to engage in productive struggle, which leads to meaning and individual learning.

The following sections explore several different instructional strategies and approaches to promote critical thinking and problem-solving skills, including questioning, brainstorming, inquiry- or problem-based learning, thinking routines, and more.

Questioning

Questioning is a familiar instructional strategy for many educators. We use questioning to gauge learners' understanding and to help them observe, explain processes, and share their ideas. Skillful questioning plays a critical role in cultivating thinking skills and deep learning. Questioning strategies can model for students how they should think and help them to develop metacognition.

Using questioning strategies intentionally in the learning environment is a core practice for promoting critical thinking skills for all learners. A good question can open learners' minds and deepen engagement with a subject matter. In education, we usually emphasize discussions where learners answer questions that we pose ourselves or derive from instructional materials. However, the most important lesson we can teach our learners is to formulate their own questions to promote critical thinking skills. Asking the kinds of questions that will encourage students to make connections, elaborate, and develop metacognition isn't necessarily an intuitive skill for educators, but the good news is that these skills can be developed.

In an inquiry classroom, for example, our questions have many different purposes, including engaging students' interest, critiquing and analyzing a particular idea, promoting divergent thinking, making connections, establishing patterns and relationships, scaffolding students' planning, problem-solving to help them figure something out for themselves, promoting reflection, and encouraging students to evaluate, self-assess, and goal set (Murdoch, K., 2015).

Brainstorming

Brainstorming can be an effective strategy to increase critical thinking skills, particularly when used in combination with techniques to create visual representations such as graphic organizers or concept maps. There are many types of graphic organizers and tools that promote learner thinking in different ways, for example, flowcharts, fishbone, or compare and contrast diagrams. These kinds of visual tools are considered *cognitive tools* because they guide learner thinking. Concept mapping—technically a graphic organizer with linking phrases describing relationships between concepts or ideas—helps learners to describe relationships and how concepts are connected. This helps learners to make critical connections, particularly when mapping concepts in response to a guiding question or task.

By regularly using sample question stems like the following, we are encouraging high levels of engagement in classrooms and helping to reinforce particular ways of thinking.

- In what ways might we improve *x*?

- What are the characteristics of *x*?

- What is it about *x* that sets it apart from other *x*'s?

- How can we do *a* and *b*? (adapted from Elkenberry, 2007).

> **TYPES OF QUESTIONS**
>
> How can educators differentiate between different types of questions? Check out this helpful classification of question types from the Harvard Graduate School of Education's Project Zero (qrgo.page.link/JnV7u). For critical thinking, focus on questions which are generative, constructive, or facilitative.
>
>

Brainstorming sessions can be productive to encourage genuine collaboration and interaction among all learners in the classroom while promoting critical thinking and problem-solving skills.

Inquiry-Based or Problem-Based Learning

Creating opportunities in the classroom where learners can select which topics or questions to explore, and encouraging questions from learners contributes to higher levels of learner engagement and motivation. While involved in their own chosen in-depth studies, learners have opportunities to ask probing questions that encourage deep thinking and help them distinguish between relevant and irrelevant information. Curiosity and questioning are important characteristics of critical thinkers as they approach inquiry with an open mind.

For inquiry-based learning, teachers will need to change their focus to a more interactive approach, where learners are doing most of the talking and teachers are lecturing less. Learners will feel more independent and self-directed (Stearns, 2017). A focus on inquiry allows them to use their curiosity to guide their questions and their ongoing learning. "Teachers are the architects for learning. They design the environment for developing minds" (Erikson, 1995, p. 181) therefore, teachers need to create classrooms of inquiry where learners are aware that thinking is crucial and they are all supported in their learning journey to be critical thinkers and problem solvers.

Thinking Routines and Thinking Roles

Project Zero's initiative, Visible Thinking, explores the impact of creating simple but impactful thinking routines to scaffold and deepen learning. By making thinking visible and by sharing mental processes and models, we can examine and understand them. The Project Zero thinking routines were developed to be easy to

remember, simple to use, and applicable across contexts. For example, the think-puzzle-explore routine "has students share what they think about a topic, identify questions they puzzle about, and target directions to explore" (Ritchhhart & Perkins, 2008, p. 57). The team has developed several other thinking routines such as see-think-wonder and connect-extend-challenge. Learn more about these routines by scanning the QR code or visiting tiny.cc/h1x67y.

An effective strategy for promoting flexible thinking is to assign roles. Learners assume the roles, then apply or direct thinking. In a study, 4th and 5th grade students were trained in thinking roles: task definer, strategist, monitor, and challenger. As a result, learners "earned superior retention scores on three variables when compared with control children. The variables included the use of self-directed thinking skills, amount of information used in solution, and quality of answer" (Riesenmy, Ebel, Mitchell, & Hudgins, 1991, p. 14).

Additional Strategies and Approaches

Here are more instructional strategies and pedagogical approaches that contribute to strengthening critical thinking and problem-solving skills:

- Create peer-led discussion groups.
- Design reflective assignments that encourage students to think for themselves.
- Design learning experiences to help students make connections and distinguish patterns.
- Activate learners' prior knowledge.
- Utilize flexible grouping in the classroom environment.
- Elicit learner thinking through creation of learning products.
- Use formative assessments to uncover learner misconceptions that may interfere with new knowledge building.

In the future, our learners will attempt to solve problems that we currently cannot conceptualize. By intentionally teaching critical thinking and problem-solving skills through the design thinking process, we are equipping learners with tools they will be asked to use throughout their lives.

Technologies and Digital Tools

There are many technology options and digital tools and for promoting critical thinking. It's important to remember, however, that the crucial differentiators of which technologies are appropriate for the task are the instructional applications and underlying learning design principles. When we think of the types of tools suitable for promoting learners' critical thinking, expensive options such as robotics, 3D printing and design, computer programming, digital games, adaptive software, or other specialized tools may come to mind. While technology-rich options can be engaging and exciting for learners, it's important to remember that low or no-tech options are viable and essential for our colleagues working in these teaching contexts. Key differentiators are the instructional design, learning outcomes, and pedagogical approach of the design. To promote critical thinking, digital tools and technologies should engage learners in higher-order thinking skills such as decision making, creating arguments from evidence, inference, problem identification, and generation of possible solutions.

As part of the LITE framework, educators need to be purposeful about using digital tools and technologies—including tools for video creation, formative assessment, makerspace technologies, digital games, coding, and computational thinking—that specifically support critical thinking and problem-solving skills for all learners. The following are examples of effective digital tools and technologies that can help students develop these skills. These options can be implemented relatively quickly, used at scale, and adapted to a variety of levels or content areas.

Video Creation Tools

Creating quality video responses as summaries or presentations can help learners organize and think through information critically, helping with retrieval and memory consolidation. There are many free digital tools for creating video, including low-tech options such as recording from laptops or cellphones. Storyboarding, where learners plan out the sequence of their presentation, is powerful in developing critical thinking, particularly when paired with substantive

TEACHERS THINK: VIDEO CREATION TOOLS

Students love to use Flip Grid to create videos when practicing their fluency. These videos are visible to their peers, who then leave feedback and encouraging comments and likes. This allows students to not only listen to others read, but also critique the reading behaviors they see in each video in order to understand the habits of effective readers.

When students feel they have mastered a topic in math, they are encouraged to use Screencast-O-Matic to create their own reteach video. These videos are shared with their peers, who then have the option to view the video in order to learn more about the concept. It's an effective and exciting way to engage students in metacognition.

—MEGAN C., 4TH GRADE TEACHER (mcrocker@joliet86.org)

feedback. Suggestions for digital suitable digital tools include: Google slides, PowToon, Powerpoint, Edpuzzle and FlipGrid. In addition to enhancing learning with memory retrieval practice, video content with words leverages the principles of dual coding and non-linguistic representation. For further suggestions for effective digital tools, check out this great collection from CommonSense.org (qrgo.page.link/qNfZK).

Formative Assessment

Formative assessment, which many educators implement as quick checks of understanding, not only informs instructional practice but, by prompting learners to retrieve stored information, helps to form strong connections to content, enhancing deep learning.

Critical thinking is enhanced by applying digital tools for formative feedback to support retrieval practice and when asking learners to evaluate answers—their own and others'. For example, Polleverywhere or PearDeck are great tools for formative assessment but also for discussion of the results. Asking learners where they see themselves in the data and why others may have differing points of view promotes the skills of judgment and evaluation. Check out the resources in this list of formative assessment tools from PB Works for more ideas (qrgo.page.link/VXKLm)

TEACHERS THINK: FORMATIVE ASSESSMENT TOOLS

Students read a short story in a book, but I cut out the ending. After reading, they had to collaborate in groups to determine the end of the story. Next they had to use Go Formative to draw the ending scene and write up an explanation as to what happened. At the end, each group gave a short explanation of their thinking.

—JAMIE JANOTTA, SPANISH TEACHER (jamiejanotta89@aol.com)

Makerspaces

Developing critical thinking skills and creativity through *making* objects, solutions, or processes is effective, but must be scaffolded by appropriate design challenges. By having a problem to solve,within constraints, learners' creativity and thinking are directed toward goals or outcomes. As educators, many of us have learned that a make-whatever-you-want approach often has the opposite effect of engagement—confusion and indecision!

There are many resources for starting maker programs in schools—from programs with little or no technology to complex workshops. Agency by Design, a project

 affiliated with Project Zero (Harvard Graduate School of Education), shares outstanding projects, tools, and instructional strategies for learning through making. Explore their free resources by scanning the QR code or by visiting agencybydesign.org/explore-the-framework. It's crucial to remember that you can create design challenges using binder clips or recycled materials that are just as effective as those using 3D printers and modeling software.

Digital Games

Board games have always been associated with the application of strategies. Now, learners can engage with multiple scenarios with varying outcomes that depend on their decisions and assets acquired through purposeful gameplay. Through trial and error, exploration, and problem solving, learners can earn valuable tools or affordances (e.g., additional virtual money, health, or time) to move forward in the game.

Well-designed digital games engage the learner through the application of powerful, research-based theories of motivation and learning. When learners are deeply engaged, they are motivated to spend the time immersed in game content and tasks. Learners are also encouraged to engage in risk-free, iterative trials of problem solution. However, like any digital resource, when a game is not well designed enough to sufficiently scaffold learner growth while challenging them at the right level, learners will not be engaged. When the motivation to challenge ratio is just right, learners will persist to accomplish tasks in the game—and not necessarily because they find it fun.

Digital games provide, among other important soft skills, opportunities for decision making, collaboration, role playing, and the development of social capital. As such, games can be effective in engaging learners in *social* processes such as developing empathy (e.g., the game Spent—playspent.org), recognizing the nuances of digital citizenship (e.g., CommonSense Media's Digital Compass—commonsense. org/education/digital-compass) or creating social change (e.g., Games for Change— gamesforchange.org).

Coding and Computational Thinking

Coding can be a great way to teach learners how to deconstruct a problem into parts and to work their way through solving them. Code.org, among other organizations, has a wealth of free resources to help you get started or to challenge your students to code across the curriculum. Don't let your lack of knowledge hold back your learners—learn with them! Code.org also shares unplugged activities that help to promote the important ideas of coding without using computers.

Computational thinking helps learners to think by going through a problem-solving process, usually using digital devices to solve complex problems. For example, as educators, we may be interested in graphs and visual representations of data to help us see trends and patterns, but not as concerned with the process of constructing graphs. In this way, the digital devices are used as tools for computational thinking.

Environments

The Environments section of the LITE framework guides us in shaping a positive context for all learners to promote critical thinking and problem-solving skills. Learners bring different goals, motivations, and capacities when interacting with a learning environment. High on the list of environmental factors that promote critical thinking is having a culture of thinkers, which can be cultivated by making wondering and questioning daily habits.

TEACHERS THINK: STUDENT CHOICE

Freedom of choice is necessary for student creativity. In a high school World History course, students created a multimedia project that was used as a review guide for the Semester 2 Exam. Students could use the recommended apps or explore other options. The results were diverse and unique. The project parameters can be seen here: bit.ly/2YAettH

—MIA G., INSTRUCTIONAL TECHNOLOGY COACH, SOCIAL SCIENCE TEACHER

To create an environment that promotes critical thinking and problem-solving skills, teachers can:

- Create physical spaces in which learners can pause and think, for example, a "think tank" with bean bags or comfortable seating. Small rugs could be used to create spaces for different kinds of thinking or roles.

- Move out of the classroom when possible to promote novelty and new ways of thinking.

- Bring green plants or other living things into your classroom occasionally to promote observation of change over time or to compare characteristics.

- Create a wall or space for learners to look at failures, and then suggest ways to improve the outcomes, with evidence. For example, post design challenges for students to address over a period of time, such as weekly or monthly. Better still, have the students design the challenges!

- Experiment with different pedagogical approaches, such as the many varieties of blended learning (e.g., station rotation, flipped classroom, lab rotation).

- Model critical thinking by explaining your thinking and talking out loud. Regularly ask learners to do the same.

- Use thematic units of study that are interdisciplinary and connecting with the arts.

Access to the ideas of design, innovation, and problem solving, as well as ways of thinking and habits of mind, is an important equity issue—they should be accessible for all learners

TEACHERS THINK: BLENDED LEARNING

Blended learning allows the opportunity to incorporate all 4C's daily. My students are working together and thinking about problems (in another language—Spanish) in their hyperdocs. Critical thinking is a big part of blended learning because students are given the freedom to tackle a task independently and that requires them to really think it through.

—JAMIE JANOTTA, SPANISH TEACHER (jamiejanotta89@aol.com)

TEACHERS THINK: FLIPPING WITH VIDEOS

Have you ever heard your students' parents say, "I don't understand this math, so [insert name here] couldn't finish their homework"? This is a common problem, but I used my creativity and created videos for all of my math lessons! My students can learn at their own pace and parents can use them to help their child with homework. Check out my Youtube Channel for examples! bit.ly/2UXZYJY

HEATHER K., 5TH GRADE TEACHER (hkoc@isd109.org)

Chapter Takeaways

- Critical thinking is a set of related cognitive skills including reasoning, judgement, decision making (evaluation), and problem-solving. These skills can be developed through targeted (designed) learning experiences.

- The capacity to think critically is crucial for success in our information-rich society, in which everyone can be a producer, as well as informed consumer of content.

- Learners must have some knowledge of context, which is embedded within a perspective, to be able to think critically.

- Instructional strategies to promote critical thinking focus on inquiry, making connections, generating ideas, facilitating learner knowledge, seeking, and building.

- Thinking is slow; simple but effective thinking routines can scaffold deeper learning.

- Promoting a culture of critical thinking in the learning environment can encourage learners to create (and possibly answer) their own questions.

- A wide range of digital tools and technologies can promote critical thinking. Whether the technologies are sophisticated robotics, unplugged coding, or games, the underlying instructional design is crucial for effective learning experiences which explicitly teach critical thinking.

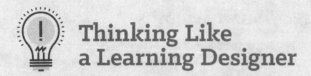

Thinking Like a Learning Designer

Promoting Critical Thinking

Moaaz is a high school technology integration specialist who is interested in promoting learners' critical thinking through social entrepreneurship and passion projects across the curriculum. He plans to engage teachers in projects to solve authentic, community-based problems through either the creation of new tools, resources, or funding.

As a first step, Moaaz asks teachers to conduct real or virtual community walks—with supporting research, such as demographics—with their learners. After a deep dive into their communities, learners are asked to observe and describe various social settings such as libraries, parks, classrooms, malls, and stores. The task is to observe for 10 minutes, then spend 15 continuous minutes describing the setting and interactions in rich detail.

Questions for Reflection

- What do you expect Moaaz' learners will observe in their communities?
- How can dialogue about observations help learners to think deeply, and to perhaps see more?
- What principles is Moaaz drawing upon in this kind of learning design?

Faith is a fourth grade classroom teacher at a K–5 school. She would like to promote critical thinking, specifically metacognitive thinking, with her young learners in her unit on energy transfer aligned with NGSS (4-PS3-2: Make observations to provide evidence that energy can be transferred from place to place by sound, light, heat, and electric currents).

Faith would like her students to use a thinking routine, specifically the Parts, Purposes, Complexities: Looking Closely sequence in which students would look at the energy transfer system and ask what are the parts, purposes, and complexities?

Questions for Reflection

- How can Faith design the instructional experience for learners by introducing thinking routines?
- What would be the benefits and drawbacks of using thinking routines for your learners?

FIELDWORK

Critical Thinking and Media Literacy

1. What does critical thinking mean to you? Reflect on Webb's depth of knowledge levels 3 and 4 (knowledge analysis and knowledge augmentation) and Bloom's levels 3 and above (analysis, evaluation, creation). Starting with one day and building to a week, track the opportunities you provide for your students to develop critical thinking and problem-solving skills. What are your instructional goals based upon analysis of your data? Resource: What EXACTLY is Depth of Knowledge? (hint: it's not a wheel) bit.ly/2TkoOnD

2. Critical thinking is crucial for media literacy and making choices about the credibility of information. According to a Stanford study (Wineburg, McGrew, Breakstone, & Ortega, 2016) released after the 2016 election "... 82 percent of middle schoolers couldn't tell the difference between a native advertisement and a news article, [but] neither could 59 percent of adults in a study conducted by the advertising industry" (Swartz, 2019). In what ways do you, or could you, increase your learners' skills to identify fake news or other false information? Resource: Snopes: www.snopes.com

Learn More:
Resources for Further Exploration

Flip Learning: *Breakout Edu: Ten Things to Know*
    (flippedlearning.org/tools_apps/breakout-edu-10-things-know)

Wabisabi Learning: *The Critical Thinking Skills Cheat Sheet* (bit.ly/2WKCZXX)

Google for Education: *Exploring Computational Thinking* (edu.google.com/resources/programs/exploring-computational-thinking)

Code.org: *Hour of Code Activities* (code.org/learn)

Hour of Code: *Coding Adventures* (playcodemonkey.com/blog/hour-of-code/coding-adventure)

Lulu: Online Self-publishing Book & eBook Company (lulu.com)

Makerspace for Education (makerspaceforeducation.com/makerspace.html)

Tynker: *Why Coding?* (tynker.com/content/why-coding)

Deep Dive

Aungst, G. (2014). *Using Webb's Depth of Knowledge to increase rigor.* Retrieved from edutopia.org/blog/webbs-depth-knowledge-increase-rigor-gerald-aungst

Beyer, B. K. (1988). Developing a Scope and Sequence for Thinking Skills Instruction. *Educational Leadership, 45*(7), 26-30.

Halpern, D. F. (2013). *Thought and knowledge: An introduction to critical thinking.* (5th Ed.) Psychology Press.

Lai, E. R. (2011). Critical thinking: A literature review. *Pearson's Research Reports, 6,* 40-41. (bit.ly/2wUlRjt)

Visible Thinking (Project Zero initiative, Harvard Graduate School of Education) (bit.ly/2IGOqGp)

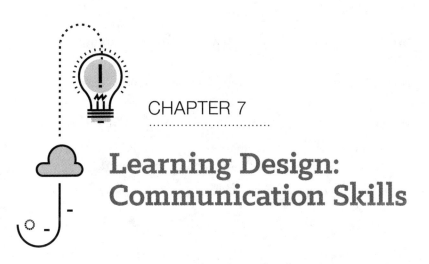

CHAPTER 7

Learning Design:
Communication Skills

We have two ears and one mouth so that we can listen twice as much as we speak.

—EPICTETUS

The difference between the right word and the almost right word is the difference between lightning and the lightning bug.

—MARK TWAIN

This chapter discusses one of the 4C's, communication. We discuss its importance for the future and the design of learning experiences to promote communication skills for all digital age learners.

By the end of this chapter, you will be able to:

- Explain the components of effective communication and its importance for learning

- Describe how effective communication manifests itself in educational settings

- Set expectations for communication using the ISTE Standards

- Design learning experiences and environments to foster the development of effective communication skills using the LITE framework

- Apply effective communication pedagogies in various contexts and for various purposes

ISTE Standards Connection

The following ISTE Standards are addressed in this chapter:

ISTE Standards for Students

6. Creative Communicator. Students communicate clearly and express themselves creatively for a variety of purposes using the platforms, tools, styles, formats and digital media appropriate to their goals.

6a. Students chose the appropriate platforms and tools for meeting the desired objectives of their creation or communication.

6b. Students create original works or responsibly repurpose or remix digital resources into new creations.

6c. Students communicate complex ideas clearly and effectively by creating or using a variety of digital objects such as visualizations, models or simulations.

6d. Students publish or present content that customizes the message and medium for their intended audiences.

ISTE Standards for Educators

6d. Educators model and nurture creativity and creative expression to communicate ideas, knowledge or connections.

ISTE Standards for Education Leaders

5d. Education leaders develop the skills needed to lead and navigate change, advance systems and promote a mindset of continuous improvement for how technology can improve learning.

Communication: Critical 21st Century Skill

Let's imagine our lives without our smartphones, Facebook, or Twitter. These innovations in the way we communicate on a daily basis show how dramatically communication has changed over the past decade. We can connect faster, with more people, in more ways than ever before. In fact, it may be necessary to entirely redefine the communication skills our students need to learn.

According to the Merriam-Webster dictionary, communication is "a process by which information is exchanged between individuals through a common system of symbols, signs, or behaviors" (2019). Communication today is much more complex and multidimensional. Ultimately, the effectiveness of any communicative endeavor is how it helps to achieve the desired outcomes. Though it is one of the 4C's of 21st century learning, we still have much to learn as the types and modes of communications continue to rapidly evolve.

Why is Effective Communication Important?

There are more demands on our learners today than any other time in history. More demands are being made on students to justify, explain, reason, and problem solve. Teachers are focusing on learners' demonstrated expertise in listening, speaking, reading, and writing in all areas of the curriculum. By focusing on developing strong communication skills for all diverse learners, we are supporting high levels of engagement and positive student learning. Strengthening all of these skills simultaneously is essential to learners' success in school and beyond.

Strong communication skills also impact the social interactions and friendships of learners. In her work with young children, professor of human development Carol Seefeldt found that,

> social skills and communication skills go hand in hand. Children who look at the child they are talking with, who understand turn-taking when communicating, and who know how to solve verbal conflicts, are those who make and keep friends easily. (Seefeldt, 2014)

We know from research that strong interpersonal skills (e.g., verbal communication, listening, decision-making and problem-solving) are critical for successful interactions and relationships and essential for effective learning. Often referred to as *soft skills*, there is increasing demand for these skills in the workplace. Educators are being asked to incorporate them into already densely packed curricula, to teach and promote deliberate practice.

We highlight conditions and strategies in this chapter that, when implemented in concert with one another, have the potential to advantage all learners to become consummate communicators, leading a more productive life.

Setting Expectations for Communication

ISTE and other organizations, such as the Partnership for 21st Century Learning (P21), have issued guidance and expectations for students' creativity in thought, communication, and design activities in order to help develop curriculum for all 21st-century learners. The ISTE standards listed at the beginning of this chapter can help guide you in designing instruction that promotes communication. As you consider the ISTE recommendations, it is important to keep in mind digital tools and technologies that can help achieve these goals.

By inference, teachers should be knowledgeable enough to guide and facilitate the development of these skills in the learning context. This expectation is expressed in the ISTE Standards for Educators Facilitator standard: "Model and nurture creativity and creative expression to communicate ideas, knowledge or connections." According to the ISTE Standards for Education Leaders, learners should be "connected" in that they develop the skills needed to lead and navigate change, advance systems and promote a mindset of continuous improvement.

Design for Communication: The LITE Framework

What are the essentials conditions for promoting communication skills? We will discuss the LITE framework: Learners, Instructional Strategies and Pedagogical Approaches, Technology and Digital Tools, and Environment in terms of the learning design for promoting strong communication skills for all learners.

Learners

Learners with strong communication skills exhibit the following characteristics:

- Exhibit excellent written and verbal skills
- Demonstrate confidence in speaking abilities
- Demonstrate competent listening abilities
- Choose their own way of demonstrating understanding
- Ask questions for clarification or elaboration
- Exhibit strong listening skills
- Convey information clearly
- Strong interpersonal skills

Learners with strong communicative competence exhibit the following skills or dispositions:

- Willingness to take intellectual risks
- Prototyping mindset, where things that don't "work" aren't wrong, but may need tweaking in application
- Problem-solving
- Divergent thinking
- Ability to transfer ideas into new contexts

Communication skills students need to have include interpersonal skills, oral and written communication skills, and the ability to read and convey nonverbal messages. Figure 7.1 lists skills that foster communication.

Instructional Strategies and Pedagogical Approaches

Instructional strategies and pedagogical approaches that support learners in their development of communication skills include:

- Developing strong presentation skills
- Asking open-ended questions
- Implementing "read aloud" activities

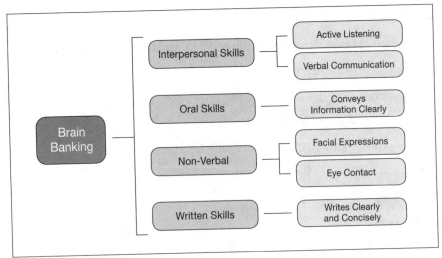

Figure 7.1 | Skills that foster communication.

- Using tasks and activities that foster critical thinking

- Implementing Think-Pair-Share active learning techniques in group discussions

- Organizing group projects

- Implementing writer's workshop strategies

Technologies and Digital Tools

There are many technologies and digital tools that support communication skills in the learner. When crafting learning experiences, it's important to consider the learner, the environment, and the instructional goal for the technology and digital tool. We will examine podcasts, school broadcasting, Skype, Google Hangout, and social media as a few of the technologies and digital tools that support, strengthen and support communication skills for all learners.

Podcasts

Podcasts are commonly described as on-demand internet radio talks. These tracks are typically audio recordings of a conversation between a host and a guest speaker, just like the ones you can listen to on the radio, or a single monologue of a person sharing his or her thoughts.

Implementing podcasting in the classroom has many educational benefits, including strengthening skills in research, writing, and collaboration—and it is easy to do. Creating podcasts can help improve students' speaking skills.

School Broadcasting

A school radio station run by and for students helps to create an inclusive environment in schools. Radio is all about communicating. Organizing a school broadcasting show takes strong communication skills to be successful. Talking to a microphone in a closed room can be less intimidating than speaking to a group. The experience of broadcasting through a school radio station builds confidence, gives students a voice, promotes working with peers.

Skype

Millions of individuals and businesses use Skype to make free video and voice calls, to send instant messages, and to share files. People can use Skype on a mobile device, computer, or tablet. Additionally, Skype is free to download and easy to use.

The use of Skype fosters the following communication skills:

- **Presence.** Students can develop presence (poise) in their communications by focusing on communicating effectively and being mindful of how they appear to others.

- **Connection and chemistry.** Individuals can learn to connect with others, both verbally and non-verbally, which can create a sense of rapport and acceptance.

- **Listening for the emotional message.** Having this skill allows individuals to set aside their own thoughts, giving others permission and psychological space to express themselves.

TEACHERS THINK: COMMUNICATION

Communication in the classroom is fostered through technology by having students consider the medium that they are using to express their ideas. For example, they might give a live verbal presentation. If they use a slide deck, they can only have a limited number of words on each slide since the focus should be on what they say. Ultimately, as social science teacher Mia G. mentioned, "there should be more images in order to guide the viewer without overwhelming them."

Social Media

Social media promotes the sharing of ideas, and information through the building of online communities—often communities of practice (ie. With other teachers working in a similar content area of grade levels). Social media is web-based and gives users quick electronic communication of content.

Environments

The design of the learning environment is critical to the development of effective communication skills of the learner. The learning environment needs to support authentic conversation and foster listening skills, questioning skills, and communication skills such as clarity, active listening, and empathy.

Environments that support strong communication skills include the following:

- Learners work at their own pace and schedule their own time

- Teachers create a supportive "community of learners," which is embedded into every aspect of classroom life.

- Learners are able to choose their assignment selections

- Talk in the classroom environment is valued by teachers and students

TEACHERS THINK: STUDENT COMMUNICATION

Running a blended learning classroom makes it that much more important to communicate with your students. I utilize Remind and Google Classroom to communicate with my students frequently. Between the messenger, and the ability to go into their Docs and make comments, my students are constantly receiving feedback and are able to ask me anything

—JAMIE JANOTTA, SPANISH TEACHER (jamiejanotta89@aol.com)

Environments that Teach Digital Citizenship

Citizenship today is digital (Krutka & Carpenter, 2017). Being a good digital citizen is critical today given the nature of digital tools, the internet, and online interactions. Digital tools can be formidable for children and it is our responsibility to make sure that all children learn how to be good digital citizens as well as have access to technology. Another important aspect of digital citizenship is teaching all learners about being safe online. Children know a lot about technology, but most do not have the maturity to navigate safely (Kivunja, 2014).

Mike Ribble (2011) in his book, *Digital Citizenship in Schools* outlines nine elements of digital citizenship: digital access, digital commerce, digital communication, digital literacy, digital etiquette, digital law, digital rights and responsibilities, digital health and wellness, and digital security.

The nine elements are grouped into three categories based on the immediacy to the typical school environment. (Ribble, 2011).

- "directly affect student learning and academic performance
- affect the overall environment and student behavior
- affect student life outside the school environment." (p. 43)

Understanding these nine elements and how they are all interconnected can help classroom teachers, technology specialists and coaches better understand the importance of digital citizenship on the environment of learning. Developing good digital citizenship requires strategies that are discussed and used daily for reinforcement (Ribble, 2011).

How can teachers, technology specialists and coaches work together to design a digital citizen curriculum in all classes for all learners in a PreK–12 school system?

Social-Emotional or Affective Factors

According to the Collaborative for Social and Emotional Learning (CASEL; casel.org) Social and Emotional Learning (SEL) is how children and adults learn to understand and manage emotions, set goals, show empathy for others, establish positive relationships, and make responsible decisions. Developing social-emotional skills is a process in which everyone practices the important life skills needed for success in all aspects of learning. Developing strong social-emotional skills at an early age is related to how competent we are socially, emotionally, academically, and professionally in our careers and later life. For example, having higher social-emotional skills in kindergarten is related to critical developmental outcomes at age 25 (Jones, Greenberg, & Crowley, 2015).

States have developed SEL standards (casel.org/csi-resources) to be incorporated as part of school curricula. CASEL's Collaborating States Initiative (CSI), launched in 2016, works with states and school districts to help develop goals, guidelines, programs, and plans that will help them promote SEL statewide. Classrooms that include SEL standards promote the principles of respect, kindness, tolerance, and empathy. When teachers focus on developing SEL skills, it affects learning by creating learning communities where children feel safe and are able to feel confident about their learning journey.

CASEL's Five Social and Emotional Competency Clusters framework identifies five core competencies:

1. Self-awareness: *I am able to identify and communicate how I am feeling.*

2. Self-management: *I can appropriately navigate my feelings.*

3. Social awareness: I *care about and respect the individual differences of others.*

4. Relationship skills: *I can handle conflict in constructive ways.*

5. Responsible decision-making: *I can predict how my behavior affects others.*

In addition, teachers can use the guides on the CASEL website (casel.org/csi-resources) to help them design supportive, caring environments for all learners.

Activities Designed to Teach Communication Skills

The activities below are designed to increase communication skills for all diverse learners.

Video-Recorded Practice for Public Speaking

Research on communication skills usually does not focus on teaching the individual skills of communication—reading, writing, listening, and speaking. Generally, the research explores teaching communication skills holistically such as reading, interpersonal communication, and public speaking. One of the areas that learners often struggle with is presentation skills or public speaking. One of the reasons is due to nervousness and anxiety when facing groups of people. A meta-analysis by Allen, Hunter, and Donahue (1989) found that the most effective approach to help anxious learners is to combine a number of elements: relaxation techniques, cognitive reappraisal to reframe the experience, and public speaking skill training in order to build confidence.

One technique that seems to be helpful in relieving the anxiety of standing up and speaking orally to a group is video-recorded practice (Rider & Keefer, 2006). When learners can see or hear themselves speak clearly on a particular topic, watching themselves can help them focus on areas that they need to improve. This practice is particularly helpful when students are provided with rubrics (Ritchie, 2016) so that they can assess themselves and their documents, and track their own growth over time. Particularly effective is combining the practice with feedback from their peers (Van Ginkel et al., 2017).

Writer's Workshop

The writer's workshop is an instructional framework that shifts the writing curriculum from focusing on the product of writing to the process of writing. Currently, we see this model implemented in learning environments across grade spans, from kindergarteners to college undergraduates, though it was used primarily in K–6 classrooms when first developed by Lucy Calkins (1994). This framework builds on students' fluency in writing through continuous and repeated experiences with the process of writing. This process ultimately impacts reading, writing, listening, and speaking skills.

During the writing workshop process, students use a daily block of time (45–75 minutes) to work on all aspects of writing. The writing process is broken into five stages: prewriting, writing, revising, editing, and publishing (sharing writing with a group). Through this approach to writing, learners manage themselves through daily writing time to develop into proficient writers.

One of the main benefits of the writers workshop model is that the materials utilized in this instructional framework are more organic and less scripted than in most writing programs. There is a prewriting stage where learners can take time to brainstorm, find ideas about what to write about, and build on those ideas. There are no workbooks because learners can choose what they write and what they are interested in, which motivates them to want to write more. Choice is an excellent motivator of learning (Graves, 1994) and choice motivates learners who struggle most, especially when it comes to writing. Also, in the last phase of the workshop, learners have an opportunity to share their writing with either a partner, small group, or the whole group. Because teachers have flexibility with sharing, they can adjust what is most productive for each group of learners. Pairing students to check each other's work gives them time to discuss together and learn from one another. When sharing and giving feedback, the *I like, I wish, I wonder* (one thing you liked about the writing, one thing you wished the writer had done differently, and one thing you wondered or question you had about the writing piece) strategy helps writers think about the process, slows down their thinking, and makes writing clearer to the reader.

By utilizing a writer's workshop model, we are promoting communication skills in a holistic learning environment, helping all learners to gain confidence in expressing themselves, and providing a supportive environment for students to ask for help from both the teacher and their peers.

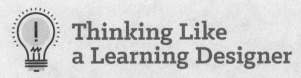

Thinking Like a Learning Designer

Communication Skills and Student Motivation

Ethan is a veteran fifth-grade teacher in a traditional school working in a diverse setting. He has a large class of 25 students, several of whom were recently diagnosed with dyslexia. Currently, he uses a traditional model of writing instruction, but according to his rubrics, as the year has progressed, his students are not increasing their writing skills. They appear unmotivated and bored, and Ethan is afraid they will give up on themselves as this frustration with writing continues. He is committed to his students and is looking for ways to change his teaching model in order to strengthen writing skills for all the diverse learners in his classroom.

Questions for Reflection

- How could Ethan begin to understand the instructional problem, looking at student work?

- From a design point of view, why do you think it would be important for Ethan to understand the students' challenges in being able to clearly communicate in their writing?

Margaret is a novice English teacher working in a diverse regional high school. She wants to create beginning-of-the-year communication activities for her freshman class. Some of her ideas include the following:

- Improve listening skills

- Watch films that model conversational skills such as body language, eye contact, summarizing, paraphrasing, responding

- Reinforce active listening

- Ask open-ended questions

She decided to begin with watching films that model conversational skills, however, the class became disinterested soon after the beginning of the film and the lesson left her and her students distracted. At the end of the school day, she felt defeated that her strategy did not work.

Questions for Reflection

- How could Margaret more effectively use films for strong conversational modeling in her classroom to help promote effective communication skills?

- What strategies could Margaret use with her students to ensure that they will be motivated to strengthen their communication skills?

Chapter Takeaways

- There are more demands on our learners today than any other time in history.

- Communication has not been given as much investigation as the other 4C's—creativity, collaboration, and critical thinking.

- Strong communication skills are connected to strong social skills, especially in the early years.

- Digital age learners need to showcase expertise as listeners, speakers, readers, and writers.

- Teachers need to provide learners with ample opportunities to interact in the learning environment in order to promote strong communication skills.

- Video-recorded practice techniques can promote strong production skills in learners.

FIELDWORK

Global Communication and Peer Evaluation

Students love learning about people from other countries. Teachers can explore academically vetted resources that allow for authentic interpersonal interactions that are supported by the use of technology.

1. Depending on learning objectives, it might be worthwhile to interact with an already established community of learners. Teachers can work together to identify and interact with individuals from a diverse set of populations. For example, students in a French class could communicate with a group of students from a city in France. Based on their backgrounds and personal interests, students could establish a relationship with a francophone correspondent of their choosing (supported by the teacher). In the event there is a language barrier, it is important that the pedagogical approach addresses both linguistic development as well as intercultural competence.

2. Design a mini writing peer evaluation using small-scale social media platform such as Twitter. Students convey messages with a limited character count and their peers will evaluate the conciseness of their message. Teachers can debrief in class and provide guidance to communicating in a clear and effective manner.

Learn More:
Resources for Further Exploration

School Radio—Let's Listen (schoolradio.com/benefit)

The Self-Expression Center: *Coaching by Phone & Skype from Anywhere in the World* (bit.ly/2YDTbeC)

Investopedia: Social Media Definition (investopedia.com/terms/s/social-media.asp)

Skills You Need: *Principles of Interpersonal Communication* (skillsyouneed.com/ips/principles-communication.html)

Batelle for Kids: Partnership for 21st Century Learning (battelleforkids.org/networks/p21)

National Educational Association: *Preparing 21st Century Students for a Global Society: An Educator's Guide to the "Four Cs"* (nea.org/assets/docs/A-Guide-to-Four-Cs.pdf)

Ephrata Area School District Innovative Learning Projects: Critical Thinking Rubrics (bit.ly/2XaRAvr)

Mindvalley: *The Podcast Beginner's Guide* (bit.ly/2YLU7O8)

Deep Dive

Communication in the 21st Century Classroom [Lynda.com elearning course]
(bit.ly/2ZYFfsa)

Intrator, D. (2016). *Communication skills are key to 21st-century success.* Retrieved from
https://thecreativeorganization.com/communication-skills-and-success

Mattson, K. (2017) *Digital Citizenship in Action—Empowering Students to Engage in Online
Communities.* International Society for Technology in Education.

Ribble, M. (2017). *Digital Citizenship: Using Technology Appropriately.* Retrieved from
www.digitalcitizenship.net/nine-elements.html

Ross, D. (2017). *Empowering our students with 21st-century skills for today.* Retrieved from
www.gettingsmart.com/2017/04/empowering-students-21st-century-skills

The University of Vermont. (2014). *How to improve communication skills in
a digital world.* Retrieved from learn.uvm.edu/blog/blog-business/
improve-communication-skills

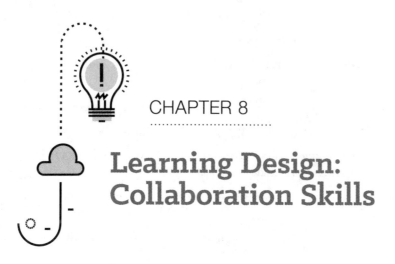

CHAPTER 8

Learning Design:
Collaboration Skills

Many ideas grow better when transplanted into another mind than the one where they sprang up.

—OLIVER WENDELL HOLMES

It takes two flints to make a fire.

—*Louisa May Alcott*

This chapter discusses one of the 4C's, collaboration. We discuss its importance for the future and the design of learning experiences to promote students' communication skills for digital age learners.

By the end of this chapter, you will be able to:

- Understand what collaboration is.

- Describe three essential skills for collaborative learning: listening, posing questions, and interpersonal skills.

- Describe how effective collaborative learning appears in classroom settings.

- Set expectations for collaboration using the ISTE Standards.

- Design learning experiences and environments to foster the development of collaborative learning skills using the LITE framework.

- Apply effective collaborative learning strategies in various contexts and for multiple purposes.

- Create complex activities that are challenging and engaging for all diverse learners.

ISTE Standards Connection

The following ISTE Standards are addressed in this chapter:

ISTE Standards for Students

2. Digital Citizen. Students recognize the rights, responsibilities, and opportunities for living, learning and working in an interconnected digital world, and they act and model in ways that are safe, legal and ethical.

7. Global Collaborator. Students use digital tools to broaden their perspectives and enrich their learning by collaborating with others and working effectively in teams locally and globally.

ISTE Standards for Educators

1. Learner. Educators continually improve their practice by learning from and with others and exploring proven and promising practices that leverage technology to improve student learning.

4. Collaborator. Educators dedicate time to collaborate with both colleagues and students to improve practice, discover and share resources and ideas, and solve problems.

STE Standards for Education Leaders

2. Visionary Planner. Leaders engage others in establishing a vision, strategic plan and ongoing evaluation cycle for transforming learning with technology.

> **2b.** Education leaders build on the shared vision by collaboratively creating a strategic plan that articulates how technology will be used to enhance learning.

> **3c.** Education leaders inspire a culture of innovation and collaboration that allows the time and space to explore and experiment with digital tools.

What Is Collaboration?

There are three fundamental characteristics of collaborative learning, which have been summarized in the definition given by OECD (2013). For the purpose of the PISA 2015 CPS assessment, collaborative problem-solving competency is defined as the capacity of an individual to effectively engage in a process whereby two or more agents attempt to solve a problem by sharing the understanding and effort required to come to a solution, and pooling their knowledge, skills and effort to reach that solution. The definition incorporates three core collaborative problem-solving competencies:

- Establishing and maintaining shared understanding

- Taking appropriate action to solve the problem

- Establishing and maintaining team organization.

For a collaborative "state" to be constructed (Brna, 1998), there have to be at least two people to share resources. Roschelle and Teasley (1995) broadly define collaboration as a "coordinated, and synchronous activity that is the result of a continued attempt to construct and maintain a shared conception of a 'problem'" (p. 70) and Dillenbourgh (1999) defines collaboration as "situation in which two or more people learn or attempt to learn something together." (p. 1). Collaboration has also been described as a skill that encourages learning mechanisms (such as induction, deduction, and associative learning) to be enacted (Dillenboug 1999, Hunter, 2006).

Collaborative Learning

Education practices have changed dramatically over the past twenty years, moving from a teacher-directed classroom to one where students are learning in small flexible groups throughout the day. School life has become group life, requiring learners to collaborate on projects, assignments, presentations, project-based learning, and small peer-led groups. Schools are also experimenting with changes in the length and structure of the school day, year-round schooling models, different forms of instruction, and transforming classroom libraries into makerspaces and idea labs. These are just some of the current innovative practices being implemented in 21st century schools to provide students with a more collaborative learning environment, where students are learning to work together effectively.

These changes require a mind shift for all 21st century educators as they design learning environments for PK–21 learners. While changing school environments, adopting innovative curriculum and working on projects in teams is improving education for 21st Century learning; educators need to intentionally examine the landscape of the classroom to design effective learning spaces that will promote social learning and maximum engagement.

Collaborating with team members in schools and communities and designing collaborative learning models is primarily rooted in Vygotsky's (1962) sociocultural theory, which is associated with children's development and construction of knowledge.

Social interaction plays a fundamental role in the process of cognitive development. In contrast to Jean Piaget's understanding of child development (in which development necessarily precedes learning), Vygotsky felt social learning precedes development.

Current PK–21 educational practice already includes group-based learning experiences, which requires strong collaboration skills. We know that these skills have an impact on the success we experience in all different types of group situations—in school, social settings, and more organized civic organizations. Designing collaborative learning activities in our learning environments will prepare learners to be part of a team, ultimately helping them succeed in their future endeavors.

We are going to examine three essential skills that are necessary for effective collaboration in the learning environment where learners work together to solve problems: effective listening, asking questions, and strong interpersonal skills.

Effective Listening

Competent listening skills are critical in all learning environments, school and otherwise. Margaret Wheatley (2002) says, "One of the easiest human acts is also the most healing. Listening to someone. Simply listening. Not advising, or coaching, but simply and fully listening" (p. 3). By explicitly improving listening skills (both our own as the teacher and that of our students), we will create a more collaborative learning space in our classrooms.

Complex activities require effective and engaged listening to understand issues and formulate optimal solutions. It is also valuable to employ constructive note-taking strategies. Jotting down a few important notes during a small group discussion helps keep the group engaged in meaningful conversation. This is important as we help learners develop their listening skills.

Asking Questions

Besides working on effective listening skills when involved in collaborative learning, another important skill to model is asking questions to explore and specify thinking. Questions may be asked for a variety of reasons—exploring ideas and assumptions and inviting others to inquire into their thinking.

Strong Interpersonal Skills

Strong interpersonal skills are critical to promoting a culture of collaboration in the classroom environment where teams successfully work together towards a common goal. Simply having learners engage in group work doesn't necessarily strengthen interpersonal skills. As noted by Rotherham and Willingham (2010), giving learners experience working in small groups is not the same as having learners practice their collaboration skills; practice implies "noticing what you are doing wrong and formulating strategies to do better" (Rotherham and Willingham, 2010, p. 19). However, this can be accomplished by receiving feedback from a more skilled teacher or peer.

Effective Collaborative Learning in the Classroom

Collaboration skills are critical for today's 21st Century learners. Our students will be required throughout their careers to work in teams and solve problems together with colleagues. To prepare these learners to be equipped for the workplace, we need to break down the essential components of collaboration skills in our classrooms so that we can intentionally teach them "what true collaboration looks like." Designing opportunities in classrooms for all learners to develop collaborative skills (i.e., strong communication, teamwork, ability to compromise) is essential for the 21st century workforce.

Design for Collaboration: The LITE Framework

What are the essential conditions for promoting collaboration in the learning environment? The LITE framework can assist educators in designing learning experiences and environments to foster the development of collaborative learning skills.

Learners

Collaboration skills students need to have include interpersonal skills, oral and written communication skills, and the ability to read and convey nonverbal messages. Figure 8.1 lists skills that foster collaboration.

Students who excel at collaboration exhibit the following characteristics:

- Possess strong interpersonal skills
- Ask high-level questions
- Have strong communication skills
- Are good active listeners
- Are good problem solvers who see the big picture and the small details
- Give and receive feedback
- Acknowledge the opinions of others
- Enjoy working with a team
- Are flexible
- Support and respect others
- Are committed to completing projects

It is important to consider what learners need to do in order to promote collaboration skills. Learners need to:

- Demonstrate the ability to work effectively and respectfully with diverse learners

- Exercise flexibility and willingness to be helpful in making compromises to accomplish a common goal

- Demonstrate effective listening skills, pose questions to explore and

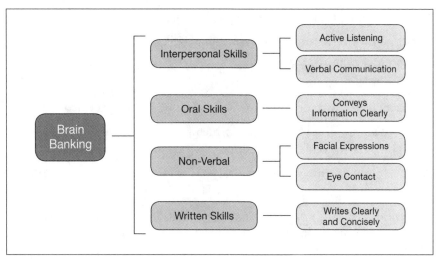

Figure 8.1 | Skills that foster collaboration.

specify thinking

- Assume shared responsibility for collaborative work

- Value individual contributions made by each team members

Learners with strong collaborative competence exhibit the following skills or dispositions:

- Willingness to work effectively and respectfully with diverse learners

- Willingness to be helpful in making necessary compromises to accomplish a common goal

- Interpersonal communication

- Ability to acknowledge and resolve disagreements

- Ability to set goals

- Ability to organize tasks

Instructional Strategies and Pedagogical Approaches

The following strategies and pedagogical approaches contribute to strengthening collaborative skills:

- Create peer-led groups in the learning environment.

- Focus on the development of interpersonal skills.

- Use brainstorming techniques (questions to be asked, issues to be solved, problem solving strategies).

- Use team learning to prompt discussions before watching a video.

- Use both ad-hoc groups with varying memberships and more permanent base groups with stable memberships in a learning environment.

- Analyze group learning processes and timing of group work in a learning environment.

- Design units of study on effective communication techniques, intentionally teaching exchanging information and productive conversations (School Outfitters, n.d.)

Technologies and Digital Tools

As part of the LITE framework, educators need to be purposeful about using effective digital tools and technologies that specifically support collaboration skills for all learners. The following examples are tools that can help achieve these goals for developing and supporting collaboration skills.

Google Drive and Dropbox

Document sharing tools such as Google Drive and Dropbox allow students to collaborate on written and presentational tasks in a way that facilitates the process of working together in a seamless way. Whether it's a written document or a PowerPoint presentation, students can load the file into Google Drive and individuals can make real-time, simultaneous contributions (such adding content, cutting and pasting text, rephrasing language) without having multiple files floating around on various devices. Students, as well as the instructor, can keep track of changes that were made in order to ensure that there is a fair distribution of efforts towards the project.

Learning Management Systems

Learning management systems (LMS) are excellent tools for collaborations involving the entire class. Two features in particular, the discussion board and the "grouping tool," use technology to increase learning opportunities in the online space and beyond. With the discussion board, students can share ideas, opinions, and answers to discussion questions in a low-risk environment that allows for deeper reflection as they are submitting their comments in writing. Students

TEACHERS THINK: COLLABORATIVE ACTIVITIES

A tic tac toe grid is one way my students collaborate in my classroom. Some requirements were a phone recording between a doctor and a patient, a video of a wellness checkup, and a fictional video presentation of owners of a company suggesting ways to maintain good health (physical and mental) to their employees. They had to work with each other (and me) throughout the entire project.

—JAMIE JANOTTA, SPANISH TEACHER (jamiejanotta89@aol.com)

reading the comments can take the time to process the information and develop their ability to evaluate the opinions of others. The "grouping tool" (which is available in most LMS) uses technology to provide a variety of ways to create mixed aptitude groups for group projects. For example, teachers can select an "automatic" setting to randomly assign students to small groups. Or the teacher can create groups manually to ensure that certain students work together. On a project that asks more responsibility of the students, they can self-select their groups and create their own course of action.

Wiki Pages

Wiki pages are another tool, like Google Drive, that allow for collaborative participation on one ultimate objective. The difference with wiki pages is they provide a space for web publication so that students can collaborate on projects such as definitions of words, encyclopedia style entries, and other educational material that is studied and then created by the class. Students can use the information that they created on the wiki pages to study for more traditional assessments that are administered throughout the year (such as a paper and pen test). The instructor can even refer to the wiki pages to inform the process of developing assessments should she be working on a unit in which standardized testing is not required.

Environments

Environments that that support collaborative learning skills:

- Create spaces where learners can comfortably work together in small groups.

- Focus on modeling effective communication skills with the entire school community, parents, staff, teachers

- Create grade level working teams in school environments to collaborate regarding curriculum, learners, technologies, professional development opportunities

- Establish professional learning communities (PLC's) in schools. These groups of educators who meet regularly to work on school or department related tasks can foster collaboration

Activities Intentionally Designed for Collaboration

Promoting real student collaboration takes time to do well. This process doesn't happen overnight, and yes, it can be challenging. Here are examples of activities intentionally designed using strategies from the LITE model to promote student collaboration.

Creating Complex Activities

One meaningful way to strengthen student collaboration is to create complex activities that are both challenging and engaging. These activities require "positive interdependence" (Johnson, Johnson & Holubec, 2008), a situation in which attaining a goal, completing the task, being successful, and getting good grades requires that the team work together and share knowledge. Designing rigorous projects that require discussion, debate and working together as a team increases learners' collaboration skills.

Prepare Learners to Be Part of a Team

We have to help learners understand the what, why and how of collaboration as part of a team for them to be successful working together in learning environments. One way to do this is to assess learners in being effective group members both individually and as a group (Johnson, Johnson & Houlbec, 2008). For example, an individual quiz can be administered based on the intended learning objectives of the collaborative activity. This way all learners are receiving individual and valuable feedback. Also, teachers can design learning inventories to help learners reflect on their own listening skills, learn about their own bias, likes and dislikes, and understand what it means to be a team member.

Build Opportunities for Discussion into the Learning Environment

It is important to foster situations in which students can work together to discuss topics and safely incorporate the variety of opinions that might be asserted about those topics. Putting students in small groups allows them to feel more comfortable voicing their opinions. Students can also work in small groups to develop an opinion in favor of one particular point, and then be directed to another small group to argue and debate that point with students who have differing opinions. Done in a respectful way, this can help students realize that it is okay for people to have differing viewpoints and that there is value in sharing their viewpoints in order to come to a general consensus in a larger group. Simulating this kind of interaction in small group settings helps students to become more comfortable with the same kind of interaction on a larger scale.

Chapter Takeaways

There has been a dramatic shift in teaching in the last twenty years from a direct instruction model for incorporating more group work practices in the learning environment.

- Collaboration is an essential skill for all learners as they prepare for a more complex global society, more collaboration is needed in the workplace.

- Listening, questioning, and interpersonal skills are all essential for effective collaboration.

- Real collaboration in the classroom environment needs to be intentionally designed by the teacher guided by the components of the LITE model

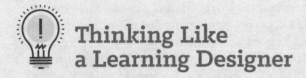

Thinking Like a Learning Designer

Peer-Led Learning

Tim is a veteran science teacher in a 6–8 middle school. He has utilized direct instruction strategies during his twenty-year teaching career. Recently he has been involved in district-level professional development regarding transforming science education through peer-led learning teams. He would like to begin implementing these peer-led teams in his current biology class. He feels that this change in his teaching would strengthen the collaboration skills of the learners in his classroom. However, he is struggling, even as an experienced teacher, with implementing a new strategy with his students in the middle of the school year. He is not sure where to start to ensure that students will be engaged in their work.

Questions for Reflection

- What are some beginning steps Tim can do to create peer-led learning teams in his classroom?

- In what ways can Tim's principal facilitate collaboration between Tim and the other science teachers in the school to help Tim create peer-led teams within his classroom?

Ellie is a new first-grade teacher at a K–5 elementary school. She has 25 kindergarten students and a part-time assistant in the afternoon. Currently, she is using a traditional reading group model (homogeneous grouping of all readers of the same level in one group). She is thinking about implementing small group discussion groups during her literacy block (reading and writing instruction). She would like to give her students more opportunities to discuss their reading books together during the Literacy block and collaborate on projects. Her professional goal this year is to implement a peer-led discussion model and invite her colleagues to observe these groups at the end of the year.

Questions for Reflection

- What are some steps Ellie can take to begin implementing peer-led discussion groups?

- What specific strategies can Ellie implement in her classroom to help her young learners become more collaborative and participate actively in peer-led discussion groups?

- Students need to collaborate and work together in the classroom on a project that is important to them so they can effectively develop and strengthen their collaboration skills.

- Creating engaging and complex activities in the classroom encourages learners to want to collaborate successfully.

FIELDWORK

Collaborating in and out of the Classroom

Students love playing games together. When students play games and/or work collaboratively, they become involved in the process, share ideas, become engaged with one another. When teachers create a collaborative culture in the classroom, this environment creates spaces where every student's strengths are valued and an environment where everyone is learning from everyone else. Teachers can explore academically vetted resources that allow for collaborative experiences that are supported by the use of technology.

1. Depending on the specific collaborative learning objective and community of learners, teachers can design opportunities in the classroom using tools like Twitter to facilitate student collaboration—bringing into the classroom something familiar which will increase student engagement and learning, making the experience more memorable for the student.

2. Teachers can also explore ways to make it easier for students to work together outside of the classroom environment, allowing more time for in-class activities. Some student collaboration tools to consider include:

   - Cacoo: Collaborative mind map creation (cacoo.com)

   - Miro: Online visual collaboration tools (miro.com)

Learn More:
Resources for Further Exploration

NEA: *Educators Guide to the 4C's* (nea.org/assets/docs/A-Guide-to-Four-Cs.pdf)

Batelle for Kids: *Is there a best way to develop the 4C's in all students?* (bit.ly/2XiFzE2)

Batelle for Kids: *The 4C's research series* (p21.org/our-work/4cs-research-series)

Deep Dive

Denise, L. (n.d.) *Collaboration vs. C-Three (Cooperation, Coordination, and Communication)* (bit.ly/31xK8de)

Jackson, S. (2013). *Find out how technology promotes teamwork and collaboration in the classroom.* Retrieved from commonsense.org/education/articles/how-technology-can-encourage-student-collaboration

Leadership Preparatory. (2019). *Collaboration: One of the 4C's of 21st Century Learning.* (bit.ly/2ZkTYNs)

Natural User Interface Technologies. (2017). *Why is collaborative learning important?* (bit.ly/2MOHsVe)

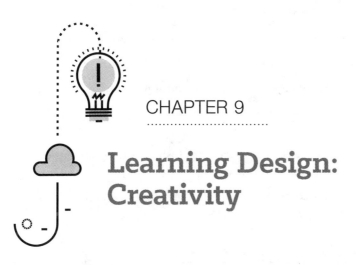

CHAPTER 9

Learning Design: Creativity

All people have creative abilities, and we all have them differently. When individuals find their creative strengths, it can have an enormous impact on self-esteem and on overall achievement.

—ALL OUR FUTURES REPORT, P. 7

Creativity is as important now in education as literacy, and we should treat it with the same status.

—SIR KEN ROBINSON

This chapter discusses the last of the 4C's, creativity. We discuss the nature of creativity, its importance for the future, and the design of learning experiences to promote creative thinking and associated skills for digital age learners.

By the end of this chapter, you will be able to:

- Recognize frameworks of creativity and their applications to learning

- Explain the role of creativity in education and the classroom

- Determine instructional approaches and methods to promote creativity

- Explore pedagogies to promote creativity in various contexts and for multiple purposes

- Design learning experiences and activities to foster the development of creative skills using the LITE framework

- Distinguish and apply components of the design thinking cycle

ISTE Standards Connection

ISTE Standards for Students

3. Knowledge Constructor. Students critically curate a variety of resources using digital tools to construct knowledge, produce creative artifacts and make meaningful learning experiences for themselves and others.

4. Innovative Designer. Students use a variety of technologies within a design process to identify and solve problems by creating new, useful or imaginative solutions.

6. Creative Communicator. Students communicate clearly and express themselves creatively for a variety of purposes using the platforms, tools, styles, formats and digital media appropriate to their goals.

ISTE Standards for Educators

6. Facilitator. Educators facilitate learning with technology to support student achievement of the ISTE Standards for Students.

> **6d.** Educators model and nurture creativity and creative expression to communicate ideas, knowledge or connections.

ISTE Standards for Coaches

2. Teaching, Learning, and Assessments. Technology Coaches assist teachers in using technology effectively for assessing student learning, differentiating instruction, and providing rigorous, relevant, and encouraging learning experiences for all students.

2d. Coach teachers in and model design and implementation of technology-enhanced learning experiences emphasizing creativity, higher-order thinking skills and processes, and mental habits of mind (such as critical thinking, metacognition, and self-regulation).

A Brief History of Creativity

Although scholars and researchers have been interested in the topic of creativity for literally centuries, until now there hasn't been a consensus on what creativity is. For educators charged with promoting creativity among their learners, it can be challenging to work without clear guidelines or parameters. In this section, we briefly discuss the evolution of ideas about the nature of creativity to provide context for these ideas.

According to Sawyer (2008), "During Plato's time (427–327 BCE) and for many subsequent centuries, creativity was perceived as divine: creativity was external to the individual" (p. 112). Creativity was considered a male pursuit that was associated with genius, almost frenzied bursts of productivity and often historically, with mental illness. Throughout history, creativity has been associated primarily with *the arts* such as painting and other fine arts, performance arts such as theater as well as writing and the humanities. It is a quality associated with talent, intellect, and gifted individuals who often think much differently than others.

Researchers J. P. Guilford and E. Paul Torrance made significant contributions to the field of study in creativity that we rely upon today. For example, the Torrance Tests of Creative Thinking (Torrance, 1974) is still used to assess creativity. Adding to our current understanding of creativity, Guilford (1950) "defined creativity in terms of two criteria: *originality* or *novelty*, and *appropriateness* or *adaptiveness*, i.e. relevance to the task at hand" (Gabora, 2013, p. 1).

For Torrance, creativity is primarily a product of *divergent thinking*, a way of thinking that generates multiple answers versus *convergent thinking*, in which the goal is to deduce the one best solution. By measuring the capacity for divergent thinking, the Torrance Tests of Creative Thinking is characteristic of viewing qualities through a *psychometric* lens (e.g., a belief that

**EXPLORE
DIVERGENT THINKING**

When your learners suggest a seemingly unrelated answer to your question, ask them to share why they think that way. Chances are, your learners may be divergent thinkers making unique connections!

creativity is an inherent, personal quality that could be measured). This implies that creativity is a *fixed* attribute that does not grow over time or experience—we are born with it in varying amounts. We now understand that creativity, like other skills and ways of thinking, can be learned and purposefully developed.

Moving forward to 1999, the National Advisory Committee on Creative and Cultural Education released an influential study by experts in creativity from diverse fields. The resulting report, "All our Futures: Creativity, Culture and Education" shared recommendations for educational policy and practice in the UK. Sir Ken Robinson, the chairperson of this committee, is a frequent speaker on schools and a renowned expert in creativity, particularly in education. His 2006 TED talk, *Do Schools Kill Creativity?*, remains one of the most watched TED talks of all time, with several million views. One of Robinson's main ideas is that children are born creative but, as they grow older, this creativity is removed through the effects of schooling, with the encouragement to conform within school contexts.

Even now, popular culture continues to propagate the idea that creative people are out of the norm, rare, extraordinarily talented, and exceptional—even quirky! The truth is, we can *all* be creative—as learners, artists, scientists, social workers, and designers. Creativity is a way of thinking built upon a set of skills that can be practiced and developed. That's great news because with the continuing, rapid pace of change, fueled by ICT and digital technologies, it's arguable that there has been no era when creativity has been needed more and in all fields. Creativity is considered by many to be one of the most important 21st-century skills, essential for innovation and interdisciplinary in nature. It is vital for our future and therefore *must* be addressed in schools.

What Is Creativity?

In a 1996 interview for WIRED magazine, Steve Jobs described creativity in this way:

> Creativity is just connecting things. When you ask creative people how they did something, they feel a little guilty because they didn't really do it, they just saw something. (Parrish, 2014)

As educators, we promote, develop, guide, and assess our learners' growing abilities in creativity and creative problem solving. With this in mind, it is critical that we explore the nature of creativity and understand how to recognize and promote those skills in our teaching. This section briefly discusses theoretical models or frameworks for understanding creativity that can guide us in our thinking of how we might design ways to develop creativity in all of our learners.

We are still discovering aspects of creativity and therefore don't have agreement around a single definition. While most of us would have difficulty in sharing a concise explanation, we could agree on the idea that creativity engages deep levels of cognitive activity and is something we can recognize when we see it.

> This lack of a common definition of creativity prevents us from having a shared understanding of the construct. Are different people even talking about the same thing when they say a certain product, idea, or artifact is more or less creative than another? (Mishra, Henricksen. & the Deep Play Research Group, 2012, p. 11)

Many theorists, however, have attempted to define creativity. For example, Professor Liane Gabora writes:

> [T]here is probably no one-size-fits-all definition of creativity. For scientific or technological enterprises, appropriateness might be more important, whereas in the arts, originality might be weighted more heavily. Thus, creativity must be assessed relative to the constraints and affordances of the task. (2013, p. 1)

She continues by describing the frequently cited 4P's of creativity—person, process, product, and place—which are helpful for educators in considering how to classifying and promote creativity in the classroom.

Peter Nilsson, a high school teacher and director of research, innovation, and outreach at Deerfield Academy, describes three domains—or regions—of creativity based on corresponding regions of perception: *material, modal,* or *mental.* According to Nilsson, "material creativity is what we most often think of when we think of creativity, either objects or behaviors" (p. 56). These are things we create out of materials, artwork for example, and we might characterize the work students do as the "creative artist or the creative child." Nilsson describes modal creativity as the act of translating the sensory experience of an object or behavior from one mode of perception to another, such as a story recreated from a verbal experience to a play or a symphony to create experiences in different modes.

Nilsson's final kind of creativity is mental creativity. He explains mental creativity as something that "we see across the curriculum." (p. 57) For example, in schools when we are teaching our subject areas (history, science, etc.), it is much more about teaching the way we understand the events—that is, their importance and implications—than it is about the events themselves. Nilsson's model is helpful for educators who would like to categorize types of creativity. Understanding the goals of learning activities is crucial to learner success—thinking of creativity in these three buckets can be a supportive lens when designing activities for promoting creativity.

Conceived by an educator, Nilsson's Taxonomy of Creative Design is an effective framework around which to discuss instructional strategies. This classification system articulates levels of creativity with increasing amounts of novelty or innovation in regards to an original work: imitation, variation, combination, transformation, and original [new] creations.

Imitation. The replication of a previous work

Variation. The modification of an existing work

Combination. The mixture of two or more works

Transformation. The translation of a work into another medium or mode

Original Creation. The creation of something previously unrecognizable (Nilsson, 2011)

Professors Mishra and Koehler, who developed the TPACK framework (discussed in Chapter 5), suggest that creativity or creative solutions have three distinct qualities: *novelty, effectiveness,* and *wholeness.* Building upon Besemer's (1998) proposal of a three-factor model of creativity, they suggest these qualities as constructs to measure the extent of creativity by evaluating the products or outcomes of creative thought because "the process of creativity is often invisible to the outsider. What we have, at the end of the day, is what the creative process produces" (Mishra & Henriksen, 2013, p. 12).

Researcher Liane Gabora proposes another view:

Although creativity is often defined in terms of new and useful products, I believe it makes more sense to define it in terms of processes. Specifically, creativity involves cognitive processes that transform one's understanding of, or relationship to, the world. (2017)

She contends that as such, there are a wide range of applications in every discipline. To be creative means to:

- Integrate novelty in products and processes

- Demonstrate insightful critical thinking and problem-solving

- Imagine something new or different

- Remix familiar ideas or materials into something new

- Design innovative solutions from within a set of constraints

Ultimately, creativity is a set of cognitive processes. Wang (2009) proposed two definitions of these processes which describe creativity as "the intellectual ability to make creations, inventions, and discoveries that brings novel relations and entities or unexpected solutions into existence," and as "a higher cognitive process of the brain at the higher cognitive layer that discovers a new relation between objects, attributes, concepts, phenomena, and events, which is original, proven true, and useful" (p. 2).

Creative thinking requires higher-order thinking and is more cognitively demanding, requiring synthesis, analysis, and evaluation. A defining characteristic of creativity is direction—creativity is a goal-directed activity. By understanding how creativity manifests itself within different disciplines, educators are better equipped to establish meaningful goals and share effective feedback to scaffold goal attainment.

For educators wishing to support the growth of creativity in their learning environments, the critical takeaway should be that there are many different ways to be creative through processes, thinking, skills, outcomes, solutions, or products. Understanding the type and level of cognitive tasks you ask of your learners—as well as the type(s) of creativity—is important in order to be able to provide meaningful scaffolding and support, to select appropriate tools, and to design effective assessment.

Creativity in Schools

In the digital age it is important to think with agility in order to solve new and ill-defined problems—problems without clear solution paths (Pretz, Naples, & Sternberg, 2003). The rapid pace of change and development necessitates creativity for continued growth. Researcher Gabora contrasts the growth and change in societal systems with biological systems: "In biological evolution, the novelty-generating components are genetic mutation and recombination... In cultural evolution, the novelty-generating component is creativity ..." when viewed through this lens; creativity is essential for continued evolution (Gabora, 2017). Her reasoning also suggests that in times of great change, creativity is a critical process to negotiate the change and subsequent adjustments—and that creativity appears differently depending upon the resources in an environment.

Despite the great need for creativity—and the growing capacity of education through digital tools and technologies to address individual learning needs—the mainstream system of schooling "is particularly ill-suited to the education of creative professionals who can develop new knowledge and continually further their own understanding" (Sawyer, 2008, p 3). According to Mishra and Henriksen, (2018),

> the most effective means to suppress creativity in modern days is schooling. In the name of education ..., modern schools have been tasked with stunting creativity and reducing individual differences. To effectively stunt creativity, modern societies have developed a sophisticated system of mechanized teaching to ensure that the compliant are rewarded and encouraged. (p. vii)

In fact, it's disappointing—and ironic—that advocacy for opportunity has resulted in a standardized education in a misguided effort toward equality. This factory inspired model of education eliminates so much by setting goals for standardized outcomes in an era of unparalleled personalized possibilities. Equity in educational opportunity should mean that each learner has support in developing their individual talents—which is not the same as equal exposure to content, despite prior knowledge, skills, and relevancy.

In the classroom, however, because of the external pressures to deliver curriculum, teachers may not recognize their creative learners—who struggle to conform. These students may ask questions that seem to challenge educators' authority, to argue or to ask off-topic questions which unintentionally derail class discussions.

Misconceptions about the nature of creativity and creative learners can impact educators' understanding and approach to instruction. Mitch Resnick (2017) describes four common misconceptions, which influence not only the classroom learning context, but also influence parents' understanding.

CONFORMITY VS. CREATIVITY

Consider the repercussions of encouraging conformity and discouraging non-compliance in your classroom. What kind of learning culture or learning ecosystem are you building—intentionally or not?

1. Creativity is [only] about artistic expression.

2. Only a small portion of the population is or could be considered creative.

3. Creativity manifests itself as a flash of insight.

4. Creativity can't be taught (and by inference—learned).

He suggests using modified language (e.g., using *creative thinking* rather than creativity) when speaking with parents to avoid confusion. It is important to have these kinds of clarifying conversations, not only with our learners and their parents and caretakers, but also to explore our colleagues' ideas about creativity and creative thinking. Another pervasive misconception that can impact the design of instructional activities is the idea that creativity means having no constraints. Often, the constraints—e.g., the robot must follow the thick black line on the mat— are drivers for creative thinking—e.g., what if it didn't?

Educators can leverage the idea of using constraints to promote creative thinking in their learners, particularly in creative problem solving. In the Fieldwork section at the end of this chapter are a couple of ideas that can be scaled throughout grade levels. The first takes a problem-based approach to literature, where learners iden- tify and propose solutions for a problem encountered in a story or reading passage. The second activity encourages creative and divergent thinking by asking students to consider alternative uses for two ordinary objects—often approached in a playful manner.

In her work on digital learning and creativity, Tufts researcher Marina Umaschi Bers talks about the importance of play to creative thought. Bers (2019) compares play within playpens to play in playgrounds as a model for promoting creativity in the classroom, particularly with digital tools and technologies such as coding:

> [P]laypens keep children safe, but they also keep them isolated. They limit their options, eliminate creative opportunities, cut off any chance of real exploration and erect physical barriers to collaboration with other chil- dren. Playgrounds, on the other hand, allow children a much greater deal of autonomy and choice. Playgrounds encourage kids to explore and play together, and create new games alone or collaborate with their peers.

While play is so crucial to learning, it is important to recognize that purposeful play is not always fun or easy. Think about the process of leveling up in learners' favorite digital games. The *productive struggle* is essential—it leads to the learning. It's easy to notice when the player perceives the task to be way beyond their proximal capabilities to learn—intense engagement turns to frustration (think ZPD!)

Design for Creativity: The LITE Framework

What are the essential conditions for promoting creativity and innovation in learning environments? The LITE framework can assist educators in designing learning activities to promote creativity in schools. We first consider learner knowledge, skills, and attitudes or dispositions.

Learners

Students need to develop many skills for creativity, especially in the areas of metacognition, self-regulation, self-efficacy, and design thinking. Consider the attributes listed in Figure 9.1 as qualities to develop within your own learners to enhance their creativity.

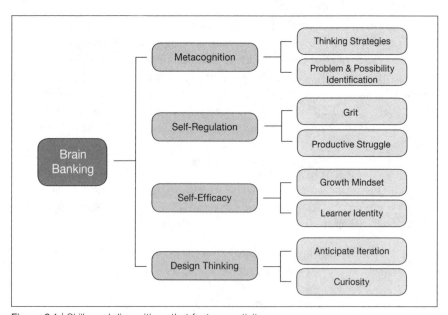

Figure 9.1 | Skills and dispositions that foster creativity.

Learners can demonstrate their growing creativity in numerous ways. For example, they:

• Are curious and inquisitive—they wonder

- Expect iterative processes where solutions are proposed, tested or analyzed, then modified or reworked (perseverance, design-thinking)

- Make connections and express original ideas

- Like to choose their own way of demonstrating their growing understanding of concepts

- Ask questions that may seem off-topic, disconnected or silly

- Like to learn through discovery and hands-on activities

- Enjoy open-ended assignments (especially older students)

- Appreciate invitations to try new ways of approaching a problem

- Need time to be reflective

- Have confidence and are able to self-identify as creative or creative problem solvers

- Enjoy being asked to imagine scenarios or outcomes

Students should have or develop the following skills or dispositions to promote creativity:

- Willingness to take intellectual risks

- Try it/prototyping mindset where things that don't work aren't wrong, but a step in solving a problem or puzzle

- Problem-solving skills and the ability to identify sources or extent of problems in particular

TEACHERS THINK: CHOICE IN LEARNING PRODUCTS

My students were given electronic game boards and could choose to complete whichever game they wanted. Some options were: write a wedding itinerary, write and record a song, create your own board game, create a presentation, and make a get well card. There were no set requirements except to show what you know, so students were able to use their creativity and they made many different versions, and they were all great!

—JAMIE JANOTTA, SPANISH TEACHER (jamiejanotta89@aol.com)

- Divergent thinking: the kind of thinking that seeks multiple solutions, instead of convergent thinking, which seeks one or two solutions

- Ability to transfer ideas into new contexts

- Understanding of how things work

- Grit: the ability to persist through challenging problems

- Are self-directed learners who know when to ask for help

Instructional Strategies and Pedagogical Approaches

Incorporating creative thinking and innovation in learning environments takes time and planning for all teachers—novice and expert alike. While we often have to work within the constraints of our district curriculums, in this section we present ideas that can be embedded into the current curriculum at almost any school to add more creativity for all learners.

Integrate the Arts

The arts have long been associated with creative expression. Not only are the arts important for self-expression, there is evidence to suggest that arts integration into curricula has lasting impact on how we encode and retain information in long-term memory. Arts integration can even be effective in teaching science: "Memories associated with arts exposure are powerful—arts experiences are thought to elicit emotional cognition, employ creative thinking pathways, and recruit cognitive processes that inherently facilitate long-term recall" (Hardiman, Johnbull, Carran, Shelton, 2019, p. 1). There is strong correlational evidence to suggest a link between arts-integrated pedagogies and long term retention of content as well as the development of key transferable non-arts related skills and important dispositions (Rinne, Gregory, Yarmolinskaya, & Hardiman, 2011). Furthermore, arts integration can support learners' emotional and mental health.

NURTURE PASSION

To effectively nurture passion, we have to have experience of it ourselves. What are you passionate about? How do your "doing" activities intersect with your passion—or not? If you had a Genius Hour or 20% Time initiative at your school, what would you work on? (for ideas, see edutopia.org/blog/five-minute-film-festival-genius-hour)

Integrate More Hands-On Learning: Making

Have you ever noticed that as a teacher, when students ask you how something should look for an assignment, many of us tend to show our best examples of a finished product? A strong element of maker culture and design thinking is the wonderful idea of acceptance—of process, imperfection, iteration, collaboration, and problem solving. Of course things don't usually work out on the first try! By removing the feeling of ineptitude and failure, making focuses on *making it happen* by working through another try with refinements—utilizing both creative and collaborative problem solving.

As educators, we are naturally reflective—we redesign on the fly, in our cars, while we are making dinner—everywhere, without consciously thinking about it. By unpacking these implicit processes, however, we can make our thoughts visible to ourselves and others—then apply these strategies purposefully and strategically. How would you deconstruct your ways of thinking and processes around iteration and modification? Think of a time when you were making or designing and had the following experiences:

1. It didn't turn out the way you wanted initially and you persisted.

2. You failed and gave up.

What's the difference between the two experiences? When did you persist? What were the conditions that enabled your success? What prompted you to give up?

Set Design Challenges

Teach your students design thinking in stages such as those shown in Figure 9.2. Involve your students in design challenges with parameters or constraints. At first, it's a good idea to suggest learners think about ideas, products, or processes that imitate others or modify existing ideas, in order to scaffold design thinking. As they gain confidence, design challenges that encourage learners to combine or transform—then to create completely new products or processes.

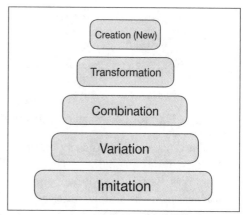

Figure 9.2 | Progression of design thinking, from simplest to most complex.

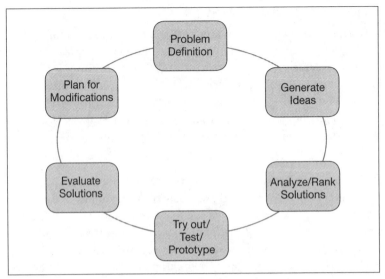

Figure 9.3 | Model for design thinking, showing cycle of processes.

Design Thinking for Creating Products and Processes

Teaching the process of design thinking is a great way to promote creative problem solving using critical thinking strategies. The model shown in Figure 9.3 represents a general perspective of a design thinking cycle and has six steps:

1. Problem definition

2. Generate ideas

3. Analyze/rank solutions

4. Try out/test/prototype

5. Evaluate solutions

6. Plan for necessary modifications

As a matter of equity and opportunity, don't shy away from making or design challenges because of an apparent lack of resources. Be creative yourself and build creativity in your learners by using simple materials such as binder clips and cardboard! Seek inspiration by watching Caine's Arcade—the story of a young maker who made his own games arcade out of cardboard (vimeo.com/40000072).

Then sign up your learners to participate in the Global Cardboard Challenge (cardboardchallenge.com)

The design thinking process begins with a deep dive to define the problem. This step is so important because poor problem definition will lead to an ineffective solution—and it may take an iteration of a cycle or two to define the actual problem.

For example, consider the problem definition process through an instructional practice lens thinking through the following outcome (or lack thereof):

Middle school learners are completing 34% of the assigned math homework.

A reasonable place to start trying to solve the problem would be to ask the students themselves why this is happening (particularly students who are not completing the assigned work). Three students respond:

1. I leave my books and materials at school (*lack of organizational skills*).

2. I don't know how to do the work (*lack of knowledge*).

3. I don't have time to complete the assignments (*poor time management*).

In considering the student responses, it may appear as if there are several potential problems to solve—organizational and/or time managements skills lacking or additional instructional support needed. It's important for us to note in this simple example that each of the different approaches to the same *problem* requires a different solution. Alternatively, there could be an overarching problem, such as poor student engagement (ineffective instructional strategies) or motivation. Working through a design process means being systematic about defining the potential problem(s) and their possible causes—then iteratively working through solutions.

Problem definition is key to the next phase of design thinking, which is to generate ideas—possible solutions—which are then ranked (by order of which to try first). Next, a prototype or draft is created, then tested and evaluated. The final phase before another iteration is planning the modifications for the next cycle. This kind of design thinking process is a flexible model. Entire iterations of the cycle could take literally minutes—or weeks, depending upon the project. The design mindset prepares learners to find a good—or the better solution, not necessarily "the best" solution. In this way of thinking, learners *expect* to cycle through possible solutions, eliminating the pressure of being *right* or *correct*.

More Ways to Promote Creative Thinking

Here is a list of tips for effective ways to promote creative thinking:

- Understand the kind of creativity you are asking of learners.

- Give learners multiple opportunities to develop metacognition and self-monitoring. Ask students how they arrived at solutions in order to develop their own metacognitive skills—thinking about their own thinking.

- Select the right cognitive objectives—those at the top of Bloom's.

- Differentiate choice of process and product to show learning.

- Encourage passion projects to develop competency and creativity.

- Engage students in social entrepreneurship—investment in issues.

- Dedicate part of the week for (approved) passion projects where students can investigate their own interests.

- Develop goals and help learners monitor their progress.

- Recognize that creativity is not a linear process.

- Ask open, probing questions.

TEACHERS THINK: STORYBOARD

Students enjoy using Storyboard to summarize their favorite myths. Once students have read a myth, they create a Storyboard project with characters, setting, and dialogue. It's a creative way to allow students to demonstrate their understanding of the text.

—MEGAN C., 4TH GRADE TEACHER (mcrocker@joliet86.org)

Technologies and Digital Tools

There are many categories of technologies and digital tools that support creativity and creative problem solving. When designing learning activities, it's crucial to understand the role and meaningful application of digital technologies to support instructional objectives. If the tech tools are fun but do not meet the learning objectives, it's analogous to creating a beautiful but non-edible cake from play dough. It may look great but without substance, it's not useful. Remember also to consider the level of cognitive objectives when designing to develop learners' creativity—be sure to be on the high end of Bloom's (Revised) Taxonomy.

Table 9.1 presents suggestions for digital tools that can be used at different steps in the design thinking cycle and the desired cognitive objective. Depending upon the instructional strategies and how the digital tools are used, teachers can leverage them as cognitive tools, that is, tools to lessen the cognitive load and maximize creative thought for problem solving.

Table 9.1. Digital Tools for Design Thinking

STEP IN THE CYCLE	COGNITIVE TASK LEVEL: Bloom's Revised Taxonomy	DIGITAL TASKS AND TOOLS
Problem definition	Remembering, Understanding	Graphic organizers, concept mapping, cognitive tools, looking up information, collecting or curating information, reviewing question and answer sites
Generating ideas / brainstorming	Remembering, Applying, Analyzing	Concept mapping, drawing tools, lists, collaborative documents and tools
Analyzing / ranking options	Analyzing, Evaluating	Specialized diagrams (e.g., fishbone) or diagramming tools, polls or quizzes, checklists, organizing
Trying out/ prototyping	Applying, Analyzing, Creating	Images, video analysis, making, design challenges, journaling, coding, CAD tools
Evaluating	Evaluating	Spreadsheets, ranking tools
Planning modifications	Creating	Journaling, reflecting, sketchnoting

TEACHERS THINK: FREEDOM OF CHOICE

Freedom of choice is necessary for student creativity. In a high school world history course, students created a multimedia project that was used as a review guide for the semester 2 exam. Students could use the recommended apps or explore other options. The results were very diverse and unique. The project parameters can be seen here: bit.ly/2FJI6x8.

—MIA G., INSTRUCTIONAL TECHNOLOGY COACH, SOCIAL SCIENCE TEACHER

Environments

In order to create learning environments that support creativity, teachers can:

- Encourage—and teach—all learners to grow in creativity and creative problem solving.

- Consider the physical environment. It shouldn't be too busy or distracting.

- Surprise your students—have a flexible furniture arrangement so that you create changes in parts of or whole classroom.

- Make the environment interesting and inviting for touch and experimentation—more like a playground than a playpen.

- Ensure learners are encouraged and supported to be independent.

- Engage in prosocial behavior. Be supportive and accepting of all learners in the learning environment.

- Allow choice in assignments, which contributes to a culture of creativity that allows for experimentation.

- Give choice in the creation of products to demonstrate learning.

- Use thematic units of study that are interdisciplinary, connecting with the arts.

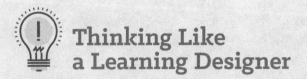

Thinking Like a Learning Designer

Creativity and Student Motivation

Jamil is a high school world history teacher working in a diverse, Title I building. He would like to design a problem-based learning experience that requires his learners to identify and suggest solutions for a problem or issue with which their communities are struggling. Jamil has asked several of his students about the project and is surprised to find them uninterested in participating. He is puzzled that his learners seem disinterested and apathetic—is this a motivation problem? An agency issue? Is there a lack of applicable skills or perhaps gaps in understanding in a problem-solving cycle?

Questions for Reflection

- What first steps could Jamil take to identify his instructional problem?

- How can Jamil work with the community to begin to bridge the disconnect between his learners and their environment?

Sara is a novice early childhood kindergarten teacher working in a Title I public school district. In her unit on monarch butterflies Sara could choose from several activities shared by her team:

- Create butterfly models from art materials

- Draw a garden to attract butterflies

- Ask students to imagine their bedroom decorated to look like a butterfly and describe it in words

- Work with a friend to demonstrate butterfly movement

- Draw a replica of a monarch butterfly to scale

Questions for Reflection

- Which activities could Sara use to promote creativity in her young learners?

- How can Sara strategically promote creativity, engage all learners, and encourage perseverance?

Chapter Takeaways

- Creativity is context-specific but usually includes elements of originality, novelty, and adaptiveness.

- Skills in creative thinking and problem solving are not set for life, they can be developed in learners.

- Using the LITE framework to design instruction can promote creativity in the classroom.

- The processes of standardization in formal schooling can discourage creativity and teachers often have biases against creative learners.

- Environments that encourage individual expression of ideas and thinking outside the box support creative thinking.

- Constraints are important—there must be a box to think outside of!

TEACHERS THINK: STORIES AND PROBLEM SOLVING

I decided to look into the story, "Muncha, Muncha, Muncha" for this activity. When I read the story, I noticed that it was about a man that was trying to protect his garden from bunnies eating his crops. Every time he would come up with a new idea to try, it would fail. But, he wouldn't give up! This book shows that making is a process that includes lots of failure and that it is okay to fail. It is actually better to fail so that you can learn from your mistakes and improve your products.

This book would also be fun to use for an actual making experience. Materials would be provided and students could work in teams, groups, or independently to find a solution to present to the class. I would inform my students that they are being recruited to help Mr. McGreely find a final solution to his "bunny" problem. I would also add the guideline that "no bunnies should be hurt in the process."

—DANIELLE GOEBBERT

FIELDWORK

Problem-Solving, Divergent Thinking, and STEAM

1. Ask learners to solve authentic problems in stories or literature. Choose your own favorite story or select a story from novelengineering.org/class-room-books, which offers sample problems and overviews. Ask students to create a solution to a problem in the story.

Ask learners to show their solution in one of these ways:

- Build it, then share pictures and details.
- Draw a detailed solution with labeled parts.

Describe how you would integrate the story, problem, and solution into a mini-lesson(s) for their peers. What criteria would you use to assess their solutions?

2. Encourage creative, divergent thinking by asking learners to juxtapose two ordinary objects to arrive at unusual uses. Choose ordinary items such as coasters, chairs, balls, a ladle, etc. Task learners to come up with ten possible uses of each item separately, then another ten, 20, or even 100 uses of the items together.

    In the beginning, learners typically stretch to think of ten uses for their items. Prompt them with questions about the function, shape, and use of the items. At first, the suggested uses are typically aligned with the objects' original purposes. As learners are prompted to consider the attributes or properties of the items, they engage in a productive struggle. After a light-bulb moment, it is almost as if the box that creates boundaries to thinking is broken—and the suggested uses that follow are more creative (and usually silly!)

    Here are some examples of objects and uses from teachers who tried this exercise:

    Coaster: lily pads for a classroom game (poly spots), Frisbee, symbols for music, weights, paint palettes, game pieces for board games, shuffleboard pieces, bookmarks (can be heavy), clays for a shooting range, fuzzy things under chairs or furniture to make sure they don't scrape the floors

    Coathanger: sword, hammer, magnifier (clear hanger), spoon to stir, fly swatter, wind chime, key rack, back scratcher, stick for fetch, scraping tool for shaping twigs or sticks

3. Demonstrate to your learners that the arts incorporate a lot of science concepts by having students participate in a STEAM art and alchemy scavenger hunt. Try this activity in your local art museum or in the class-room! Discuss one or more of the Next Generation Science Standards' crosscutting concepts (ngss.nsta.org/CrosscuttingConceptsFull.aspx). Ask students to select one outstanding example of art that demonstrates each crosscutting concept:

- Patterns

- Cause and effect

- Scale, proportion and quantity

- Systems and system models

- Energy and matter

- Structure and function

- Stability and change

Learn More:
Resources for Further Exploration

American Psychological Association: Creativity in the Classroom [videos] (apa.org/education/k12/creativity-module.aspx)

Big Think: Beau Lotto—The neuroscience of creativity, perception and confirmation bias [video] (youtube.com/watch?v=vR2P5vW-nVc)

Canva: *19 ideas to promote more creativity in your classroom* (bit.ly/2Z4bKba)

Edutopia: Critical thinking [videos] (edutopia.org/topic/critical-thinking)

Edutopia: *Getting creative with SEL* (edutopia.org/article/getting-creative-sel)

GettingSmart: *Cultivating the Culture of Creativity* (gettingsmart.com/2018/09/cultivating-the-culture-of-creativity)

Make Community: *Makerspace Playbook* (makerspaces.make.co/playbook)

TED: Brandon Rodriguez—The power of creative constraints [video] (youtu.be/v5FL9VTBZzQ)

TED: Ramsey Musallam—3 rules to spark learning (youtu.be/YsYHqfk0X2A)

TED: Andrey Vyshedskiy—The neuroscience of imagination [video] (youtu.be/e7uXAlXdTe4)

Deep Dive

Drapeau, P. (2014). *Sparking student creativity: Practical ways to promote innovative thinking and problem solving.* ASCD.

Mishra, P., & Henriksen, D. (2018). *Creativity, technology & education: exploring their convergence.* Springer.

Rinne, L., Gregory, E., Yarmolinskaya, J., & Hardiman, M. (2011). Why arts integration improves long-term retention of content. *Mind, Brain, and Education, 5*(2), 89-96.

Glossary

4C's of 21st-century learning. The 4C's of 21st- century learning, also known as the "4 C's" or "Four C's" are four skills that have been identified by the Partnership for 21st-Century (P21) as essential: critical thinking, communication, collaboration, and creativity.

Action research is a kind of practitioner research which may entail a mixture of critical, investigative, and analytical methods used by educators to study instructional problems of practice.

Adverse childhood experiences (ACEs) include all kinds of abuse, neglect, and other possible traumatic encounters that may happen to people under the age of 18, impacting their emotional growth and capacity for learning.

Agency (see learner agency)

Approaches to learning are the cognitive and emotional behaviors and skills applied by learners in the process of learning.

Associative link. When two or more events occur together but without sufficient evidence to establish that one or more brings about or causes the others.

Attention. How we actively process information in our environment, specifically focusing on selected (consciously or not) data or information while ignoring others.

Backward design is a method of designing instruction which considers goals and/or learning objectives prior to learning activities and assessments for learning.

Behaviorism theorizes that learning primarily occurs due to external influences such as conditioning (e.g. through rewards) and observation.

Brain banks. In this text, brain banks are repositories for knowledge, skills, and behaviors which promote learning.

Causative link. When strong evidence, gained through systematic (research) methods, exists that indicates one or more factors are the reason for outcomes, actions, or consequences

Cognitive load theory refers to the limited processing capacity of memory storage systems, particularly short term memory. Educators can select or create learning activities or contexts which minimize external distractions (extraneous load) to allow for greater focus upon concepts important for learning.

Cognition. The mental actions or processes of acquiring knowledge and understanding through thoughts, experiences, and input from the senses.

Cognitive science. The scientific study of human cognition including the mind, processes of thought, and learning.

Community of practice (COP). A group of people who share common interests and concerns for something they do, usually in a professional capacity. By interacting regularly, they learn from one another and explore how to improve their practice.

Concrete examples. The use of tangible, relevant (i.e., real life) examples to help learners understand abstract ideas (e.g., using manipulatives for math).

Constructivism. A theory of how people actively and individually construct their own knowledge. These views, initially posited by Jean Piaget and Lev Vygotsky, have helped shape learning approaches in today's educational landscape.

Convergent thinking. The kind of thinking in which learners seek the correct answers to questions instead of multiple possibilities.

Core practices are fundamental practices that teachers regularly enact to support learning. They consist of strategies, routines, and ways of teaching that can be deconstructed and learned.

Deliberate practice. In deliberate practice, repetition allows individuals to improve their current skills. To become an expert, simply spending hours practicing will not work—there must be deliberate practice which means that time is spent on the most effective activities to improve performance. Deliberate practice focuses on strengthening targeted weaknesses or performance deficits.

Design principles are fundamental rules of thumb based upon the learning sciences that educators may use to cultivate learner agency, assure the development of higher level skills, and design learning experiences based on the interests and needs of the learners.

Design thinking is a systematic, iterative process through which a problem is identified, possible solutions are brainstormed then tested, and the outcomes are evaluated followed by modifications. Design thinking occurs in cycles.

The digital age. The digital age is characterized by rapid technology-driven progress. The future will be full of enormous growth, but it will also be a world of immense unpredictability.

Divergent thinking is a thought process to create many possible solutions to an identified problem or consideration, in contrast to convergent thinking.

Educational psychology is the branch of psychology focused on the scientific study of human understanding in educational contexts.

Elaboration. The process of using questioning strategies in a purposeful manner, by which educators can facilitate and promote deep learning by making connections to existing knowledge.

Extrinsic motivation. Rewards or other incentives like praise, fame, or money are used to motivate learners to perform in a certain manner or for specific activities.

Fidelity of implementation refers to the degree practitioners adhere to the stated policies and procedures required for success when implementing a program, set of instructions, or learning intervention.

Fixed mindset. The notion that qualities such as intelligence are fixed attributes you are born with and are unable able to change.

Formative assessment. The process of assessment during instructional activities such as practice in order to provide feedback and direction for next steps in learning.

Goal orientation can be either learning or performance orientations and refers to the motivation for individuals to complete tasks. A learning goal orientation is more intrinsically or internally motivated whereas a performance goal orientation is aligned with external gains.

Gradual release of responsibility (GRR). A particular style of teaching which is framed around a process of developing the independence of the learner by strategically decreasing scaffolds.

Growth mindset describes the underlying beliefs people have about learning and intelligence. When students believe they can get smarter through sustained effort, they can be encouraged to persist in time and effort, leading to higher achievement.

Habits of mind are routines or ways of thinking. They are strategies or systems of learning to use when encountering new information or problems.

Heuristics are uncomplicated, systematized rules, series of steps, or routines, learned or communicated then used as strategies for problem solving during learning.

High leverage practices. Evidence-based, highly effective teaching practices that may be used across grade levels, subject areas, and contexts.

Human development refers to the biological and psychological development of the humans throughout their lifetime. It consists of the growth from infancy to adulthood.

Identity (learner identity) can broadly be described as a self-conception of learners' capacities to learn.

Inattentional blindness or **perceptual blindness** occurs when someone fails to perceive new or unexpected things that suddenly appear within their visual field, which may lead to missing important details.

Inquiry-based learning. A form of active learning that starts by posing questions, problems, or scenarios, rather than simply presenting established facts or portraying a smooth path to knowledge.

Instructional design or **instructional systems design** is based on how people learn and refers to the efficient design of instructional materials and learning contexts. Well-designed instructional materials foster cognitive processes for the learner and facilitate stronger learning outcomes.

Instructional strategies are approaches used by teachers to share instructional content and to assist students in becoming independent learners.

Interdisciplinary or **interdisciplinary studies** involves the combining of two or more academic disciplines into one activity.

Interleaving involves incorporating learning materials from multiple sources into a single study session rather than focusing on one topic or idea.

Intrinsic motivation. The reason for acting for internal satisfaction or reward versus external reasons.

Learner agency refers to learners' capacities to participate in learning processes through activities that are meaningful and relevant to learners. Learner agency also gives students voice, and often choice, in how they learn developing independence.

Learning ecology. A system including the physical, social, and cultural components of the learning context.

Learning environment. The diverse physical locations, contexts, and cultures in which students learn, such as classrooms, museums, or the workplace.

Learning identity is a key aspect of metacognitive knowledge about how one learns, particularly their views about their ability to learn. People with a positive learning identity see themselves as capable learners that seek and engage life experiences with a learning attitude and believe in their learning potential.

Learning intervention. The process of creating and applying a possible solution to an instruction problem or practice.

Learning outcomes or **learning targets** guide the learner and teachers. They are goals of instruction which distinguish the pieces of knowledge, skills, and accomplishments learners will need to know for deep understanding.

Learning science, **the learning sciences** or **the science of learning**. An interdisciplinary area of study comprised of a number of academic fields and the intersections or spaces between them. Among these fields of study are cognitive science, educational research, neuroscience, sociology, human-computer interaction, instructional technologies, linguistics, and psychology. The core principle uniting the study of these areas is an interest in the processes of individuals learning alone or in groups. Learning scientists study learning as well as engaging in the design and implementation of effective learning innovations and improving instructional methodologies. (Elkordy & Keneman, p. 1)

Learning theories characterize how students acquire, process, and retain knowledge during learning.

Linking words and phrases. Transition words used to join two or more sentences or nodes in concept mapping.

Mental models are memory structures and ideas that represent how we conceptualize or think about a topic.

Metacognition. Thinking about one's thinking—specifically, the processes or strategies of thinking. Good metacognitive skills allow leaners to mentally retrace their thinking and apply strategies to solve problems.

Motivation. The reasons why individuals act and persist in actions. Motivation is an important aspect of learning, helping learners become and stay engaged in academic tasks in order for deep learning to occur.

Multidisciplinary. Combining or involving several academic disciplines or professional specializations in an approach to a topic or problem.

Neuroeducation. An interdisciplinary field that combines neuroscience, psychology, and education to create improved teaching methods and curricula.

Neuromyth. A commonly held false belief about neuroscience or about how the brain works.

Neuroplasticity refers to the ever-changing nature of the brain as it forms connections and grows through experiences.

Neuroscience. The scientific study of the brain and supporting nervous systems.

Personalized learning seeks to augment student learning and motivate by tailoring the instructional environment—what, when, how, and where students learn—to address the individual needs, skills, and interests of each student.

Piagetian theory. Jean Piaget's theory of cognitive development and intelligence refers to children's stages as they move through four different phases of mental development. Piaget's stages are: sensorimotor: birth to 2 years, preoperational: ages 2 to 7, concrete operational: ages 7 to 11, and formal operational: ages 12 and up.

Pedagogy is the method and practice of teaching as an academic subject or theoretical concept. A pedagogical approach refers to a particular method or practice.

Pedagogical content knowledge (PCK). A type of knowledge that is unique to teachers and is based on the manner in which teachers relate their pedagogical knowledge (what they know about teaching) to their subject matter knowledge (what they know about what they teach).

Professional learning community (PLC). Professional learning communities in education aim to enhance the knowledge and skills of teachers through joint study of student growth and success as well as stronger leadership and teaching systems.

Project-based learning (PBL). An instructional framework that develops key 21st century skills. Learners collaborate in groups to complete the project. The PBL model encourages critical thinking, creativity, innovation, inquiry, collaboration, and communication.

Qualitative research is a process of inquiry that seeks an in-depth understanding of social phenomena within their natural setting. It is characterized by data collection methods which seek to record the direct experiences of human beings such as interviews, observations, and focus groups.

Quantitative research is a structured way of collecting and analyzing numerical data which may represent concepts or quantities. It is characterized by statistical analysis and data representations.

Retrieval practice involves retrieving information from long term memory. By retrieving the information and bringing it to mind, new connections can be made and memories strengthened.

Schema theory refers to the theory that long term memories are stored in schema, which are neural constructs representing how we think about a concept. New knowledge is acquired by matching prior knowledge, stored in schema, then making connections.

Self-efficacy is the degree of confidence in one's own ability to exert control over motivation, behavior, and social environment. For example, a teacher with high self-efficacy believes in their own capacity to effect deep student learning.

Self-regulation is control over one's own emotions and thoughts. It is important for learners in managing emotions and persistence.

Sense making. The process by which people give meaning to new learning and experiences. In the process, we look for prior knowledge, saved in the brain as schema, upon which to build the new information (think of it as classifying or categorizing information).

Socio-cognitive theory proposes that learning occurs within and is informed by social and cultural contexts, often by observing others.

Soft skills are those qualities that apply across a variety of careers and life situations—traits such as integrity, courtesy, responsibility, collaboration, effective communication, professionalism, and teamwork.

Social and emotional learning (SEL) includes the understanding and management of emotions, goal setting, and attainment; forming and maintain positive relationships; and interacting positively and productively with others with empathy and understanding.

Spaced practice or **distributed practice** is a learning strategy where the practice is broken up into a number of short sessions and over time so the learner practices retrieval of the information repeatedly.

Rubric. An educational scoring guide designed to evaluate the expectations of a particular skill or concept to ascertain a level of proficiency and growth over time.

Summative Assessment. An assessment designed to evaluate a particular skill or concept at the end of a learning period. It is the evaluation of student learning.

Teaching practices are the ways in which teachers discern and execute instruction. Teaching practices generally reflect educators' beliefs about the teaching and learning process.

Technological Pedagogical Content Knowledge (TPACK) is designed around the idea that content (what you teach) and pedagogy (how you teach) must be the basis for any technology that you plan to use in your classroom to enhance learning. (Mishra and Kohler, 2006)

Translational research. Research which forms a bridge between the finding and outcomes of traditional research and practical applications, eg., for learning and instruction.

Zone of proximal development (ZPD) represents the potential growth learners could acquire at the present time. Teachers who understand this idea can ensure that learners are learning slightly beyond their present skills and make accommodations with ongoing support. Teaching too far beyond individuals' ZPD can lead to frustration and demotivation.

References

Achmad, D., Bustaria, A., & Samad, I. (2017). The use of podcasts in improving students' speaking skills. *The Journal of English Education, Vol. 2* No. 3, pp. 97–111.

Aguilar, E. (2015). *Shifting mental models in educators.* Retrieved from www.edutopia. org/blog/shifting-mental-models-educators-elena-aguilar

Allen, M., Hunter, J. E., & Donohue, W. A. (1989). Meta-analysis of self-report data on the effectiveness of public speaking anxiety treatment techniques. *Communication Education, 38*(1), 54–76.

Ambrose, S. A., Bridges, M. W., DiPietro, M., Lovett, M. C., & Norman, M. K. (2010). *How learning works: Seven research-based principles for smart teaching.* New York: John Wiley & Sons.

Anderson, L. W., Krathwohl, D. R, & Bloom, B. S. (2001). *A Taxonomy for learning, teaching and assessing: A revision of Bloom's taxonomy of educational objectives.* New York: Longman.

Andreasen, N. C. (2014). *Secrets of the creative brain.* Retrieved from www.the atlantic.com/magazine/archive/2014/07/secrets-of-the-creative-brain/372299/

Armstrong, P. (2018). *Bloom's taxonomy center for teaching.* Retrieved from https://cft. vanderbilt.edu/guides-subpaes/blooms-taxonomy/

Aslaksen, K., & Lorås, H. (2018). The modality-specific learning style hypothesis: A mini-review. *Frontiers in psychology, 9,* 1538.

Barab, S., & Squire, K. (2004). Design-based research: Putting a stake in the ground. *The Journal of the learning sciences, 13*(1), 1-14.

Barnes, D. (1976). *From communication to curriculum.* Harmondsworth, England: Penguin.

Barnett, M. A. (1989). Writing as a process. *The French review, 63*(1), 31–44.

Beetham, H., & Sharpe, R. (Eds.). (2013). *Rethinking pedagogy for a digital age: Designing for 21st-century learning.* New York: Routledge.

Bers, M. U. (2019). *Make your classroom more like a playgound than a playpen using 'hard fun'*. Retrieved from www.edsurge.com/news/2019-01-08-make-your-classroom-more-like-a-playground-than-a-playpen-using-hard-fun

Blakemore, S. J., Grossmann, T., Cohen-Kadosh, K., Sebastian, C., & Johnson, M. H. (2013). Social development, (pp. 268–295) in *Educational neuroscience*. Mareschal, D., Butterworth, B., & Tolmie, A. (Eds.). New York: John Wiley & Sons.

Bloom, Benjamin S. & Krathwohl, (1956). *Taxonomy of educational objectives: The classification of educational goals, by a committee of college and university examiners. Handbook 1: Cognitive domain.* New York: Longman.

Bowen, Ryan S., (2017). *Understanding by design.* Retrieved from https://cft.vanderbilt.edu/understanding-by-design

Bransford, J., Brown, A. L., Cocking, R. R., & National Research Council (U.S.). (2000). *How people learn: Brain, mind, experience, and school. Expanded edition.* Washington, D.C: National Academy Press.

Brna, P. (1998). *Models of collaboration.* Proceedings of the Workshop on informatics in Education. XVII Congresso Nacional da Sociedade Brasileira de Coputacao, Belo Horizonte, Brazil.

Broadbear, J. (2003). Essential elements of lessons designed to promote critical thinking. *Journal of the Scholarship of Teaching and Learning*, 1–8.

Brown, A. L. (1992). Design experiments: Theoretical and methodological challenges in creating complex interventions in classroom settings. *The journal of the learning sciences, 2*(2), 141–178.

Brown, J. S., Collins, A., & Duguid, P. (1989). Situated cognition and the culture of learning. *Educational researcher, 18*(1), 32–42.

Bruner, J. (1957). *Going beyond the information given.* New York: Norton

Bruner, J. S. (1966). *Toward a theory of instruction* (Vol. 59). Harvard University Press.

Burns, M. (2019). *I'm a neuroscientist. Here's how teachers change kids' brains.* Retrieved from www.edsurge.com/news/2019-02-19-i-m-a-neuroscientist-here-s-how-teachers-change-kids-brains

California Department of Education. (n.d.). *Grade level expectations for reading writing and communicating.* Retrieved from www.cde.state.co.us/sites/default/files/documents/coreadingwriting/documents/rwc_gle_at_a_glance.pdf

Calkins, L. (1994). *The Art of Teaching Writing.* Portsmouth, NH: Heinemann.

Cambridge Assessment International Education, (n.d.) *Developing the Cambridge learner attributes.* Retrieved from www.cambridgeinternational.org/Images/417069-developing-the-cambridge-learner-attributes-.pdf

Carmichael, R., & Farrell, H. (2012). Evaluation of Effectiveness of Online Resources in Developing Student Critical Thinking: Review of Literature and case Study of Critical Thinking Online Site. *Journal of University Teaching and Learning Practice, 9*(1), 4.

CAST (2018). *Universal Design for Learning Guidelines version 2.2.* Retrieved from http://udlguidelines.cast.org

Center on the Developing Child (n.d.). *A guide totoxic stress.* Retrieved from https://developingchild.harvard.edu/guide/a-guide-to-toxic-stress

Churches, A. (2008). *Edorigami, Bloom's taxonomy and digital approaches.* Retrieved from http://coe.sdsu/eet/Articles/bloomrev/start

Chick, N. (n.d.), *Learning styles.* Retrieved from https://wp0.vanderbilt.edu/cft/guides-sub-pages/learning-styles-preferences/

Claro, S. Paunesku, D. & Dweck, C. S. (2016). *Mindset tempers effects of poverty on achievement.* Proceedings of the National Academy of Sciences Aug 2016, 113 (31) 8664-8668; DOI:10.1073/pnas.1608207113

Coalition for Psychology in Schools and Education. (2015). *Top 20 principles from psychology for preK–12 teaching and learning.* American Psychological Association.

Coffield, F., Moseley, D., Hall, E., & Ecclestone, K. (2004). *Learning styles and pedagogy in post-16 learning: A systematic and critical review.* Retrieved from www.leerbeleving.nl/wp-content/uploads/2011/09/learning-styles.pdf

Coffield, F., Moseley, D., Hall, E., & Ecclestone, K. (2004). *Should we be using learning styles? What research has to say to practice.* London: Learning and Skills Research Centre.

Collins, A. (1992). Toward a design science of education. In *New directions in educational technology* (pp. 15–22). Springer, Berlin, Heidelberg.

Cozolino, L. (2013). *The social neuroscience of education: Optimizing attachment and learning in the classroom*. New York: W. W. Norton & Company.

Cozolino, L. (2013). *Nine things educators need to know about the brain*. Retrieved from https://greatergood.berkeley.edu/article/item/nine_things_educators_need_to_know_about_the_brain

Csibra, G., & Gergely, G. (2009). Natural pedagogy. *Trends in cognitive sciences, 13*(4), 148–153.

Darling-Hammond, L. (1995). Changing Conceptions of Teaching and Teacher Development. *Teacher Education Quarterly, 22*(4), 9–26.

Davidson, C. N. (2011). *Now you see it: How the brain science of attention will transform the way we live, work, and learn*. New York: Viking.

Davis, Barbara Gross. (1993). *Tools for teaching*. San Francisco. Jossey Bass Publishers.

Dekker, S., Lee, N. C., Howard-Jones, P., & Jolles, J. (2012). Neuromyths in education: Prevalence and predictors of misconceptions among teachers. *Frontiers in psychology, 3*, 429.

Dembo, M. H., & Howard, K. (2007). Advice about the use of learning styles: A major myth in education. *Journal of college reading and learning, 37*(2), 101–109.

Dewey, J. (1997). *How we think* (Original work published in 1933). USA: Dover Publications

Dillenbourg, P (1999). What do you mean by collaborative learning? In Dillenbourg P. (ed.) *Collaborative learning: cognitive and computational approaches*. Oxford: Elsevier.

Dixon-Krauss, L. (1995). *Vygotsky in the classroom: Mediated literacy instruction and assessment*. White Plains, NY: Longman.

Drapeau, P. (2014). *Sparking student creativity: Practical ways to promote innovative thinking and problem solving*. Alexandria, VA: ASCD.

Dumont, H, Istance, D. & Benavides, F. (2010). *The nature of learning: Using research to inspire practice*. Center for Educational Research and Innovation. Retrieved from www.oecd.org/education/ceri/thenatureoflearningusingresearchtoinspirepractice.htm

Dweck, C. S. (2008). *Mindset: The new psychology of success*. New York: Random House.

Elkenberry, K. (2007). *Brainstorming strategies: Seven questions that spur better solutions.* Retrieved from: www.sideroad.com/Meetings/brainstorming.pdf

Elkordy, A. (2016). *Digital badges for STEM learning in secondary contexts: A mixed methods study.* Retrieved from https://commons.emich.edu/theses/809

Erickson, H. (1995). *Stirring the head, heart and soul.* Thousand Oaks, CA: Corwin.

Ferrance, E. (2000). Themes in education: Action research. *Educational Alliance, 34*(1).

Fissler, P., Kolassa, I. T., & Schrader, C. (2015). Educational games for brain health: revealing their unexplored potential through a neurocognitive approach. *Frontiers in psychology, 6*, 1056.

Fogarty, R. J. (n.d.). *7 Critical thinking skills of Common Core.* Retrieved from www.iaase.org/Documents/Ctrl_Hyperlink/Session_30_7_Critical_Thinking_Skills_of_Common_Core_uid9152013500282.pdf

Forehand, M. (2005). *Bloom's Taxonomy: Original and revised.* Retrieved from http://projects.coe.uga.edu/epltt/

Futures, A. O. (1999). *Creativity, Culture and Education.* National Advisory Committee on Creative and Cultural Education (NACCCE). Retrieved from: http://sirkenrobinson.com/pdf/allourfutures.pdf

Gabora, L. (2013). Psychology of creativity. In Elias G. Carayannis (Ed.) *Encyclopedia of Creativity, Invention, Innovation, and Entrepreneurship* (pp. 1515–1520). New Delhi, India: Springer.

Gabora, L (2017). *What creativity really is—and why schools need it.* Retrieved from http://theconversation.comwhat-creativity-really-is-and-why-schools-need-it-81889

Gagné, R. M., & Newell, J. M. (1970). *The conditions of learning.* New York: Holt, Rinehart & Winston.

Gee, J. (2004). *Situated language and learning: A critique of traditional schooling.* New York: Routledge.

Glaser, R. (1976). Components of a psychology of instruction: Toward a science of design. *Review of educational research, 46*(1), 1–24.

Graves, D. (1994). *A fresh look at writing.* Portsmouth, NH: Heinemann.

Greeno, J. G. (1989). A perspective on thinking. *American Psychologist, 44,* 134–141.

Greeno, J.G. (2006), "Learning in Activity", in R.K. Sawyer (ed.), *Cambridge Handbook of the Learning Sciences.* Cambridge University Press, pp. 79–96.

Goodwin, B. (2018). *Student learning that works: How brain science informs a student learning model.* Denver, CO: McREL International.

Gutiérrez, K. D., & Rogoff, B. (2003). Cultural ways of learning: Individual traits or repertoires of practice. *Educational researcher, 32*(5), 19–25.

Halpern, D. F. (1996). *Thought and knowledge: an introduction to critical thinking* (5th ed.). New York, NY: Psychology Press.

Hardiman, M. M. (2012). *The brain-targeted teaching model for 21st-century schools.* Thousand Oaks, CA: Corwin Press.

Hardiman, M. (2012). Informing pedagogy through the brain-targeted teaching model. *Journal of Microbiology & Biology Education: JMBE, 13*(1), 11.

Hardiman, M. M., JohnBull, R. M., Carran, D. T., & Shelton, A. (2019). The Effects of Arts-Integrated Instruction on Memory for Science Content. *Trends in Neuroscience and Education.*

Hart, L. A. (2002). *Human brain and human learning* (3rd edition). Covington, Washington: Books for Educators.

Hasso Plattner Institute of Design at Stanford. (2007). *Design thinking process.* Palo Alto, CA: Stanford University

Hattie, J. (2008). *Visible learning: A synthesis of over 800 meta-analyses relating to achievement.* New York: Routledge.

Hattie, J. (2017), *Visible learning plus 250+ influences on student achievement.* Retrieved from https://visible-learning.org/wp-content/uploads/2018/03/VLPLUS-252-Influences-Hattie-ranking-DEC-2017.pdf

Hirsch, E. (2019). *4 years and 500+ reports later.* Retrieved from www.edreports.org/resources/article/anniversary

Heritage, M. (2008). *Learning progressions: Supporting instruction and formative assessment.* Retrieved from www.michigan.gov/documents/mde/CCSSO_Learning_Progressions_Mararget_Heritage_1_601110_7.pdf

Hunter, D. (2006). Assessing collaborative learning. *British Journal of Music Education, 23*(1), 75–89.

Immordino-Yang, M. H., & Damasio, A. (2007). We feel, therefore we learn: The relevance of affective and social neuroscience to education. *Mind, brain, and education, 1*(1), 3–10.

Interstate New Teacher Assessment and Support Consortium. (2013). *InTASC: Model core teaching standards and learning progressions for teachers 1.0.* Washington, DC: Council of Chief State School Officers.

International Society for Technology in Education. (2017). *ISTE standards for educators.* Arlington, VA: International Society for Technology in Education.

Ito, M., Gutiérrez, K., Livingstone, S., Penuel, B., Rhodes, J., Salen, K., ... & Watkins, S. C. (2013). *Connected learning: An agenda for research and design.* BookBaby.

Jonassen, D. H. (1999). Designing constructivist learning enviroments: Instructional design theories and models: *A new paradigm of instructional theory, 2*, 215–239.

Johnson, D. W. Johnson, R. & Holubec E. (2008). *Cooperation in the classroom.* Minneapolis, MN: Interaction Book Company.

Johnson, J. (2015). *How might educators use operant conditioning to direct classroom behavior and learning?* Retrieved from www.quora.com/How-might-educators-use-operant-conditioning-to-direct-classroom-behavior-and-learning

Jones, D. E., Greenberg, M., & Crowley, M. (2015). Early social-emotional functioning and public health. *American Journal of Public Health 105*, 11, pp. 2283–2290.

Kail, R. V. & Cavanaugh, J. C. (2008). *Human development: A life-span perspective* (5th ed). Cengage Learning

Kim, H., McGivney, E. & Care, E. (March 28, 2017). *Science of learning: Why do we care?* Retrieved from www.brookings.edu/blog/education-plus-development/2017/03/28/science-of-learning-why-do-we-care/

Kirschner, P. A. (2017). Stop propagating the learning styles myth. *Computers & Education, 106*, 166–171.

Kivunja, C. (2014). Innovative Pedagogies in Higher Education to Become Effective Teachers of 21st-century Skills: Unpacking the Learning and Innovations Skills Domain of the New Learning Paradigm. *International Journal of Higher Education 3*(4), 27–48.

Kolb, L. (2017). *Learning First, Technology Second: The Educator's Guide to Designing Authentic Lessons.* Arlington, VA: ISTE.

Krathwohl, D. R. (2002). A revision of Bloom's taxonomy: An Overview. *Theory and Practice, 41*(4), 212–218.

Lai, E. R. (2011). *Motivation: A literature review research report.* Retrieved from https://images.pearsonassessments.com/images/tmrs/Motivation_Review_final.pdf

Lange, S. (2014). *Strategies to Promote Critical Thinking in the Elementary Classroom.* Retrieved from https://learningfirst.org/blog/strategies-promote-critical-thinking-elementary-classroom

Laurillard, D. (2013). *Teaching as a design science: Building pedagogical patterns for learning and technology.* New York: Routledge

Laal, M. & Ghodsi, S. M. (2012). Benefits of Collaborative Learning. *Procedia-Social and Behavioral Sciences, 31*, 486–490.

Lieberman, D. A., Fisk, M. C., & Biely, E. (2009). Digital games for young children ages three to six: From research to design. *Computers in the Schools, 26*(4), 299-313.

Lucariello, J., & Naff, D. (2012). *How do my students think: Diagnosing student thinking.* Retrieved from: www.apa.org/education/k12/student-thinking.aspx

McCarthy R. & Pittaway, S. (2014). Historical Exploration of Creativity Research. In *The Future of Educational Research: Bold Visions in Educational Research.* Rotterdam: Sense Publishers.

McCroskey, J.C. & McCroskey, L. L. (1988). Self-report as an approach to measuring communication competence. *Communication Research Reports, 5*(2), 108-113.

McEwan B. & Guerrero, L. K. (2010). Freshman engagement through communications: Predicting friendship formation strategies and perceived availability of network resources from communication skills. *Communications studies, 6*(14), 445-463.

Madda, M. J. (2017). *Kids don't fail, schools fail kids: Sir Ken Robinson on the 'Learning Revolution.'* Retrieved from www.edsurge.com/news/2017-02-23-kids-don-t-fail-schools-fail-kids-sir-ken-robinson-on-the-learning-revolution

Mandinach, E. (2019). *Understanding educational psychology.* Retrieved from www.apa.org/action/science/teaching-learning

Marzano, R. J., Gaddy, B. B., & Dean, C. (2000). *What works in classroom instruction.* Aurora, CO: Mid-Continent Research for Education and Learning.

Mayer, R. E. (2003). *Learning and instruction.* Upper Saddle River, NJ: Merrill.

Mareschal, D., Butterworth, B., & Tolmie, A. (Eds.). (2013). *Educational neuroscience.* New York: John Wiley & Sons.

Masterman, L., & Vogel, M. (2007). Practices and processes of design for learning. *Rethinking pedagogy for a digital age.* Beetham, H. & Sharpe, R. (eds). (52–63). New York: Routledge

Masterman, L. (2013). The challenge of teachers' design practice. In *Rethinking pedagogy for a digital age.* Beetham, H. & Sharpe, R. (eds). (pp. 88–101). New York: Routledge.

Mendelson, T., Greenberg, M. T., Dariotis, J. K., Gould, L. F., Rhoades, B. L., & Leaf, P. J. (2010). Feasibility and preliminary outcomes of a school-based mindfulness intervention for urban youth. *Journal of abnormal child psychology, 38*(7), 985-994.

Miller, G. A., Galanter, E. & Pribram, K. H. (1960). *Plans and the structure of behavior.* New York: Holt, Rinehart & Winston.

Mishra, P., & Koehler, M. J. (2006). Technological pedagogical content knowledge: A framework for teacher knowledge. *Teachers college record, 108*(6), 1017.

Mishra, P., & Koehler, M.J. (2008). *Introducing technological pedagogical content knowledge.* Paper presented the Annual Meeting of the American Educational Research Association, New York, March 24-28.

Mishra, P., & Henriksen, D. (2018). *Creativity, technology & education: exploring their convergence.* New York: Springer.

Mishra, P., Henricksen, D., & Deep-Play Research Group. (2013). Rethinking technology & creativity in the 21st century. *TechTrends, 57*(3), 10-14.

Mitchell, P. (2016), *From concept to classroom: What is translational research?* Retrieved from research.acer.edu.au/cgi/viewcontent. cgi?article=1009&context=professional_dev Australian Council for Educational Research, Camberwell VIC 3124

Murdoch, Kath. (2015). *The power of inquiry: Teaching and learning with curiosity, creativity, and purpose in the contemporary classroom.* NY: Seastar Publishing Co.

National Academies of Sciences, Engineering, and Medicine. (2018). *How people learn II: Learners, contexts, and cultures.* Washington, DC: National Academies Press.

National Research Council. (2012). *A framework for K–12 science education: Practices, crosscutting concepts, and core ideas.* Washington, DC: National Academies Press.

National Research Council. (2018). *How people learn II: Learners, contexts, and cultures.* Washington, DC: National Academies Press.

National Research Council. (2000). *How people learn: Brain, mind, experience and school. Expanded edition.* Washington, DC: National Academies Press.

Nilson, L. B. (2016). *Teaching critical thinking: Some practical points.* Faculty Focus. Retrieved from www.facultyfocus.com/articles/effective-teaching-strategies/ teaching-critical-thinking-practical-points

Nilsson, P. (2013). *The cognitive science of education.* Retrieved from www. senseandsensation.com/2013/03/cognitive-science-next-education.html

Nilsson, P. (2011). The Challenge of Innovation. In *Critical Thinking and Creativity: Learning Outside the Box.* Paper presented at the Proceedings of the 9th International Conference of the Bilkent University Graduate School of Education, Ankara, Turkey: Bilkent University.

OECD (2008) *Understanding the brain: The birth of a learning science—New insights on learning through cognitive and brain science.* Retrieved from www.oecd.org/site/ educeri21st/40554190.pdf

OECD (2013). *Programs for International Student Assessment* (PISA) 2015; Draft Collaborative Problem Solving Framework. Retrieved from www.oecd.org/pisa/pisaproducts/Draft%20PISA%202015%20Collaborative%20 Problem%20Solving%20Framework%20.pdf

Papert, S.A. (1971). *Teaching children thinking.* Retrieved from hdl.handle. net/1721.1/5835

Pashler, Harold, McDaniel, M., Rohrer, D., & Bjork, R. (2008). Learning styles: Concepts and evidence. *Psychological Science in the Public Interest. 9.3,* 103-119

Paul, R., Elder, L., & Bartell, T. (1997). *Study of 38 public universities and 28 private universities to determine faculty emphasis on critical thinking in instruction.* Retrieved from www.criticalthinking.org/pages/study-of-38-public-universities-and-28-private-universities-to-determine-faculty-emphasis-on-critical-thinking-in-instruction/598

Paul, R. and Elder, L. (2006). *The art of socratic questioning.* Dillon Beach, CA: Foundation for Critical Thinking.

Piaget, J. (1971a). The theory of stages in cognitive development. In D. Green, M. P. Ford, & G. B. Flamer (Eds.), *Measurement and Piaget* (pp. 1e11). New York: McGraw-Hill.

Ponterotto, J. G. (2006). *Brief note on the origins, evolution, and meaning of the qualitative research concept "thick description".* Retrieved from www.nova.edu/ssss/QR/QR11-3/ ponterotto.pdf

Pretz, J. E., Naples, A. J., & Sternberg, R. J. (2003). Recognizing, defining, and representing problems. *The psychology of problem solving, 30*(3).

Pritchard, A. (2018). *Ways of learning (4th edition).* New York: Routledge.

Puentedura, R. (2010). *SAMR and TPCK: Intro to advanced practice.* Retrieved from hippasus.com/resources/sweden2010/SAMR_TPCK_IntroToAdvancedPractice.pdf

Quinn, R. E., Heynoski, K., Thomas, M., & Spreitzer, G. M. (2014). *The best teacher in you: How to accelerate learning and change lives.* Retrieved from http://www.doc88.com/p-8148932070733.html

Ratna, S., & Tron, B. (2015). *Learning theories: Implications in teacher education.* Retrieved from www.academia.edu/6730061/ Learning_Theories_Implications_in_Teacher_Education

Rauscher, F. H., & Hinton, S. C. (2006). The Mozart effect: Music listening is not music instruction. *Educational Psychologist, 41*(4), 233-238.

Reigeluth, C. M., Merrill, M. D., & Bunderson, C. V. (1978). The structure of subject matter content and its instructional design implications. *Instructional science, 7*(2), 107-126.

Resnick, M. (2017). *4 myths about creativity*. Retrieved from www.edutopia.org/article/4-myths-about-creativity

Ribble, M. (2011). *Digital citizenship in schools, Second edition*. Eugene, OR: International Society of Technology in Education.

Rider, E. A. & Keefer, C. H. (2006). Communication skills competencies. Definitions and a teaching toolbox. *Medical Education, 40*(7), 624-629.

Riener, C., & Willingham, D. (2010). The myth of learning styles. Change: *The magazine of higher learning, 42*(5), 32-35.

Riesenmy, M. R., Ebel, D., Mitchell, S., & Hudgins, B. B. (1991). Retention and transfer of children's self-directed critical thinking skills. *The Journal of Educational Research, 85*(1), 14-25.

Rinne, L., Gregory, E., Yarmolinskaya, J., & Hardiman, M. (2011). Why arts integration improves long-term retention of content. *Mind, Brain, and Education, 5*(2), 89-96.

Ritchhart, R., & Perkins, D. (2008). Making thinking visible. *Educational leadership, 65*(5), 57.

Ritche, S. M. (2016). Self- assessment of video-recorded presentations. Does it improve skills? *Active learning in Higher Education. 17*(3), 207-221.

Robinson, Ken. (2006). *Sir Ken Robinson: Do schools kill creativity?, TED Ideas Worth Spreading*. Retrieved from www.ted.com/talks/ken_robinson_says_schools_kill_creativity?language=en

Rodgers, D. (January 19, 2018). *The TPACK Framework Explained (With Classroom Examples)*. Retrieved from www.schoology.com/blog/tpack-framework-explained

Rogoff, B. (1990). *Apprenticeship in thinking*. New York: Oxford University Press.

Rose, D.H., and Meyer, A. (2002). *Teaching every student in the digital age: Universal Design for Learning*. Alexandria, VA: Association for Supervision and Curriculum Development.

Rotherham, A. J. & Willingham, D. T. (2010). 21st-Century skills: not new, but a worthy challenge. *American Educator, Spring*, 17-20.

Ryan, R. M. and Deci, E.L. (2000). Intrinsic and extrinsic motivations. Classic definitions and new directions. *Contemporary Educational Psychology, 25,* 54-67.

Sawyer, R.K., (2008). *Optimising learning: Implications of learning sciences research.* Organization for Economic Co-operation and Development, Centre for Educational Research and Innovation, pp. 45, 35-98.

Schinkten, O. (2017). *The best tech tools for getting students to think critically.* Retrieved from learning.linkedin.com/blog/education/the-best-tech-tools-for-getting-students-to-think-critically

Schunk, D. H. (2012). *Learning theories an educational perspective, Sixth edition.* New York: Pearson.

Seefeldt, C. (n.d.). *Helping children communicate: Early childhood today.* Retrieved from www.scholastic.com/teachers/articles/teaching-content/helping-children-communicate

Sergis, S., Papageorgiou, E., Zervas, P., Sampson, D. G., & Pelliccione, L. (2017). Evaluation of Lesson Plan Authoring Tools Based on an Educational Design Representation Model for Lesson Plans. In *Handbook on Digital Learning for K–12 Schools* (pp. 173-189). New York: Springer.

Shuell, T. J. (1986). Cognitive conceptions of learning. *Review of educational research, 56*(4), 411-436.

Simon, H. A. (2000). Observations on the sciences of science learning. *Journal of Applied Developmental Psychology, 21*(1), 115-121.

Simons, D., & Chabris, C. (1999). *Selective attention test.* Visual Cognition Lab: University of Illinois. Retrieved from youtu.be/vJG698U2Mvo

Skinner, B. F. (1938). *The Behavior of Organisms: An experimental analysis.* New York: Appleton-Century.

Smith, T. (July 2, 2012). *Writing measurable learning objectives.* Retrieved from teachonline.asu.edu/2012/07/writing-measurable-learning-objectives

Smith, M. & Weinstein, Y. (2016). *Strategies for Effective Learning: For teachers, for students, for researchers, for parents, learning scientists posts.* Retrieved from www.learningscientists.org/blog/2016/8/18-1

Snyder, L. G., & Snyder, M. J. (2008). Teaching critical thinking and problem-solving skills. *The Journal of Research in Business Education, 50*(2), 90.

Sousa, D. A. (2017). *How the brain learns.* (Fifth edition) Thousand Oaks, CA: Corwin.

Stearns, S. (2017). What is the place of lecture in student learning today? *Communication Education, 66*(2), 243-245.

Sternberg, R. (2006). The nature of creativity. *Creativity Research Journal, 18*(1), 87-98

Swartz, K. (2019). *How to teach students historical inquiry through media literacy and critical thinking.* Retrieved from www.kqed.org/mindshift/53123/how-to-teach-students-historical-inquiry-through-media-literacy-and-critical-thinking

Sweller, J. (1994). Cognitive load theory, learning difficulty, and instructional design. *Learning and instruction, 4*(4), 295-312.

TeachingWorks, (2018). *High leverage teaching practices.* University of Michigan. Retrieved from www.teachingworks.org/work-of-teaching/high-leverage-practices

Thille, C. (2016). *Bridging learning research and teaching practice for the public good: The learning engineer.* TIAA Institute. Retrieved from origin-www.tiaainstitute.org/sites/default/files/presentations/2017-02/bridging_learning_research_and_teaching_practice.pdf

Tokuhama-Espinosa, T. (2018). *Neuromyths: Debunking false ideas about the brain.* New York: WW Norton & Company.

Tokuhama-Espinosa, T. (2017). *The difference between mind, brain and education, educational neuroscience and the learning sciences.* Retrieved from www.youtube.com/watch?v=nAGsJ3xP944

UNESCO. (n.d.). *The silk road.* Retrieved from en.unesco.org/silkroad/about-silk-road

Van Ginkel, D. Guilkers, J. Blemans, H. & Mulder, M. (2017). Fostering oral presentation performance: Does the quality of feedback differ when provided by teachers, peers, or peers guided by tutors? *Assessment & Evaluation in Higher Education, 42*, 953-966.

Vygotsky, L. S. (1978). *Mind in society: The development of higher psychological processes.* Cambridge, MA: Harvard University Press.

Vygotsky, L. S. (1976). *Thought and language* (A. Kozalin, Trans.) Cambridge, MA: MIT Press. (Original work published 1934).

Wagner, T. (n.d.), *Tony Wagner's seven survival skills*. Retrieved from www.tonywagner. com/7-survival-skills

Wang, Y. (2009). On cognitive foundations of creativity and the cognitive process of creation. *International Journal of Cognitive Informatics and Natural Intelligence (IJCINI), 3*(4), 1-18.

Wang, F., & Hannafin, M. J. (2005). Design-based research and technology-enhanced learning environments. *Educational technology research and development, 53*(4), 5-23.

Watson, J. B. (1930). *Behaviorism* (rev. ed). Chicago: University of Chicago Press.

Weinstein, Y., Sumeracki, M., & Caviglioli, O. (2019). *Understanding how we learn: A visual guide*. New York: Routledge.

Weinstein, Y., Madan, C. R., & Sumeracki, M. A. (2018). Teaching the science of learning. *Cognitive Research: Principles and Implications, 3*(1), 2.

Wenger, E. (2011). *Communities of practice: An introduction*. Retrieved from www.uwoakville.org/wpv3/wp-content/uploads/2013/12/Communities-of-Practice-introduction-document.pdf

Wiggins, G., & McTighe, J. (2005). *Understanding by design.* Alexandria, VA: ASCD.

Wheatley, M. (2002). *Turning to one another. Simple conversations to restore hope to the future.* San Francisco, CA: Berrett-Koehler.

Williamson, J. (2015). *Effective digital learning environments: Your guide to the ISTE standards for Coaches.* Eugene, Oregon: International Society for Technology in Education.

Willingham, D. T. (2005). Do visual, auditory, and kinesthetic learners need visual, auditory, and kinesthetic instruction. *American Educator, 29*(2), 31-35.

Willingham, D. T. (2007). Critical thinking: Why it is so hard to teach? *American Federation of Teachers, Summer 2007,* p. 8-19.

Willingham, D. T. (2009). *Why don't students like school?: A cognitive scientist answers questions about how the mind works and what it means for the classroom.* New York: John Wiley & Sons.

Willingham, D. T. (2010). Have Technology and Multitasking Rewired How Students Learn? *American Educator, 34*(2), 23.

Willingham, D. (2018). *Does tailoring instruction to "learning styles" help students learn?* Retrieved from www.aft.org/ae/summer2018/willingham

Willingham, D. T., Hughes, E. M., & Dobolyi, D. G. (2015). The scientific status of learning styles theories. *Teaching of Psychology, 42*(3), 266-271.

Willis, J. (2006). *Research-based strategies to ignite student learning: Insights from a neurologist and classroom teacher.* Alexandria, VA: ASCD.

Willis, J. (2014). Neuroscience reveals that boredom hurts. *Phi Delta Kappan, 95*(8), 28-32.

Wineburg, S., McGrew, S., Breakstone, J. & Ortega, T. (2016). *Evaluating information: The cornerstone of civic online reasoning. Stanford digital repository.* Retrieved from http://purl.stanford.edu/fv751yt5934

Yang, Y. T. T., & Wu, W. C. I. (2012). Digital storytelling for enhancing student academic achievement, critical thinking, and learning motivation. A year-long experimental study. *Computers & Education, 59* (2), 339-352.

Yates, G. C., & Hattie, J. (2013). *Visible learning and the science of how we learn.* New York: Routledge.

References

Index

Your Opinion Matters
Tell Us How We're Doing!

Your feedback helps ISTE create the best possible resources for teaching and learning in the digital age. Share your thoughts with the community or tell us how we're doing!

You Can:

- Write a review at amazon.com or barnesandnoble.com.

- Mention this book on social media and follow ISTE on Twitter @iste, Facebook @ISTEconnects or Instagram @isteconnects

- Email us at books@iste.org with your questions or comments.